DATE DUE FOR RETURN

**This book may be recalled
before the above date**

90014

D1439047

ROYAL HISTORICAL SOCIETY

STUDIES IN HISTORY 50

REPRESENTATIVES OF THE LOWER CLERGY IN PARLIAMENT 1295–1340

REPRESENTATIVES OF THE LOWER CLERGY IN PARLIAMENT 1295—1340

Jeffrey H. Denton and John P. Dooley

THE ROYAL HISTORICAL SOCIETY

THE BOYDELL PRESS

© J. H. Denton and J. P. Dooley 1987

First published 1987

Published for the Royal Historical Society by
The Boydell Press
an imprint of Boydell & Brewer Ltd
PO Box 9   Woodbridge   Suffolk IP12 3DF
and Wolfeboro NH 03894-2069, USA

UK ISBN 0 86193 207 2

British Library Cataloguing in Publication Data
Denton, Jeffrey
Representatives of the lower clergy in Parliament,
1295–1340. — (Royal Historical Society studies in
history series, ISSN 0269-2244 ; no. 50)
1. Great Britain. *Parliament. House of Commons*
— History 2. Clergy — Great Britain — Minor
orders — History 3. Legislators — Great Britain —
History
I. Title II. Dooley, J.P. III. Royal Historical Society
IV. Series
328.41'073   JN515
ISBN 0-86193-207-2

Library of Congress Cataloguing-in-Publication Data applied for

Printed in Great Britain by
St Edmundsbury Press, Bury St Edmunds, Suffolk

Contents

The Society records its gratitude to the following whose generosity made possible the initiation of this series: The British Academy; The Pilgrim Trust; The Twenty-Seven Foundation; The United States Embassy's Bicentennial funds; The Wolfson Trust; several private donors.

Preface

We offer this study, which has developed out of an M.A. thesis by J. P. Dooley (Manchester, 1980), in the belief that there are occasions when the former work of researcher and supervisor may be transformed with benefit into a co-operative venture. Professor C. R. Cheney and Dr Alison K. McHardy kindly commented in detail upon early drafts of the work, and we gratefully record our debt to them. We wish to thank, too, Dr Dorothy Clayton and Dr Peter McNiven, of the John Rylands University Library, for their unfailing kindness and efficiency, and Dr Patrick Mussett and Dr Meryl R. Foster for their generous help with manuscripts at Durham. Documents in the Appendices are published by permission of the Dean and Chapter of Durham, the Dean and Chapter of Lincoln, the British Library Board and the Controller of H.M. Stationery Office. The book is dedicated to all the authors of undergraduate and postgraduate theses arising out of the Special Subject on Edward I's reign, taught in the University of Manchester between 1970 and 1982.

J.H.D.
J.P.D.
August 1984

Abbreviations

Abbreviated titles used in the footnotes can be found in the Select Bibliography.

BIHR	*Bulletin of the Institute of Historical Research*
BJRL/BJRUL	*Bulletin of the John Rylands (University) Library*
BL	British Library, London
Bodl.	Bodleian Library, Oxford
CRO	Cumbria Record Office
CUL	Cambridge University Library
CYS	Canterbury and York Society
D. & C.	Dean and Chapter
EDR	Ely Diocesan Records
EHR	*English Historical Review*
HMC	Historical Manuscripts Commission
HMSO	Her Majesty's Stationery Office
HWRO	Hereford and Worcester Record Office
LAO	Lincolnshire Archives Office
LI	Lincoln's Inn, London
LPL	Lambeth Palace Library, London
LRO	Lichfield Joint Record Office
PRO	Public Record Office, London
RS	Rolls Series
SRO	Somerset Record Office
WRO	Wiltshire Record Office

1

Introduction

Study of the emergence of the English parliament has often, quite naturally, focused upon the duties and powers of the elected representatives. In the course of the thirteenth century communities — whether the communities of lower clergy, shires, burgesses or merchants — were able through their chosen proctors to obtain a degree of representation in royal assemblies of the individual rights of free men, so that, on the one hand, obligations to royal government could be fulfilled and, on the other hand, local or particular interests defended. Anyone undertaking to discuss representation in the middle ages must be mindful of the fact that the notion was often used to affirm the status of the monarch. The natural frame of reference for the examination of representation by legists or theologicans was political unity.[1] Whether the two counterweights — the application of royal authority and the defence of the rights of communities — should be assessed apart from each other, at any stage in the early development of representative assemblies, is altogether doubtful. Even so, judging the force of the one factor in relation to the other lies at the heart of all analyses of the origins and development of parliament. Of crucial significance, therefore, has been the study of the powers which communities granted, in response to the royal summons, to their representatives. The discussion has centred upon the elected laymen from shire and borough courts.[2] Yet, for the first century of parliament's history,

---

[1] See Michaud-Quantin, *Universitas*, pp. 305—26 and G. de Lagarde, 'L'idée de représentation dans les oeuvres de Guillaume d'Ockham', *Bulletin of the International Committee of Historical Sciences*, 9 (1937), 425—51.

[2] See, notably, Edwards, *'Plena potestas'*, which was criticised in Post, *'Plena potestas* and consent'. And see below pp. 16—17, 37—9. Nowhere does Post suggest that the Crown was 'merely' obeying the imperatives of Roman law in summoning representatives to come with full power to act: cf Prestwich, 'Parliament and community', p. 9.

very much more evidence has survived concerning the powers of the elected representatives of the lower clergy in parliament. The clerical proctors have escaped close attention[3] largely because their rôle in parliaments — though not, of course, in provincial convocations — declined, apparently to insignificance, during the latter part of the fourteenth century. The development of a lay commons — and of the parallel but distinct convocations of Canterbury and York — has acquired an aura of inevitability. But the attempt, during the period 1295 to 1340, to bring the lower clergy into parliament was one of the first major experiments in parliamentary practice. To ignore the experiment because it failed is to miss the opportunity to comprehend more fully the nature of parliamentary representation in the late thirteenth and early fourteenth centuries. An inquiry into the whole process of the appointment by the parish clergy and by the cathedral clergy of men to represent them in sessions of the highest court of the realm will not only shed light on the status and views of the lower clergy. It will also enable us to understand more clearly what was distinctive about the lay representatives sent by counties and boroughs.

If we are to talk of 'members of parliament' during the early period of the development of parliament, we can hardly exclude the representatives of the lower clergy. Only by a long and gradual process did the clergy below the prelates completely withdraw from parliamentary assemblies. The principle — embodied in the *Modus Tenendi Parliamentum* — of the bringing together in parliament of the communities of clergy and laity certainly died hard.[4] Whatever

---

[3]   Two works of the early eighteenth century are still of some importance: Atterbury, *Rights, Powers and Privileges* and Wake, *State of the Church*. Of recent works see especially Lowry, 'Clerical proctors', Clarke, *Representation*, McHardy, 'Representation of clergy', Denton, *'Communitas cleri'* and *idem*, 'Clergy and parliament'. Dooley, 'The lower clergy in parliament 1295–1340' includes, pp. 76–181, full transcripts of most of the letters of proxy in the PRO listed in Appendix 5 below.

[4]   See especially the section 'De clero' of the *Modus: Parliamentary Texts*, ed. Pronay and Taylor, pp. 67–8. The introductory remarks by Pronay and Taylor concerning the clergy in parliament (pp. 23, 25, 41–3) must be read with care. The claim of a difference between the two versions of the *Modus* concerning the summoning of the clergy (p. 25 n. 46) seems impossible to substantiate. And there is no justification for the statements (derived, in part at least, from B. Wilkinson, *Constitutional History of Medieval England*, III (London, 1958), 381) that clerical proctors ceased to attend parliament 'after about 1322' or 'after 1330' or

the origin and date of the English *Modus*,[5] it expressed in this respect a notable political ideal of the fourteenth century. It is well to remember the message of the section of the *Modus* concerned with the granting of aids to the king. The author stated that there could be no parliament at all without the presence of the clerical and lay communities, even if all the archbishops, bishops, earls and barons, and their peers were present with the king. He continued:

> It is necessary that all matters which ought to be confirmed or annulled, granted, denied, or done by parliament, ought to be granted by the community of parliament, which is composed of three grades or orders of parliament, that is to say the proctors of the clergy, the knights of the shire, the citizens and burgesses, who represent the whole community of England, and not the magnates because each of these is at parliament for his own individual person, and for no one else.[6]

In examining the relationship of the lower clergy with the English Crown as illustrated by the rôle of their representatives, it is important to have in mind, at the outset, the areas of study on which this subject impinges. Given the nature of the sources it is hardly surprising that scholars have devoted more attention to the higher clergy than to the lower. We have seen, of late, the publication of a number of books concerned with the careers of particular archbishops and bishops of this period,[7] and no doubt there will be more studies of the kind, illuminating *inter alia* the links between

---

'after about 1332' (*Parl. Texts*, ed. Pronay and Taylor, pp. 23, 25 & n. 46). The date 1332 appears to stem from a misunderstanding of statements made in Clarke, *Representation*, pp. 20, 126, 146. Clarke did not actually believe that attendance ceased in the 1330s: 'There was certainly no dramatic secession of proctors' (p. 126). It is, however, true that there is no reference to the proctors of the lower clergy on the rolls of parliament after 1332: see *Rot. Parl.*, II. 64b, 65b as cited in Clarke, *Representation*, p. 20.

5 For the argument that it was composed in Richard II's reign see G. O. Sayles, 'Modus Tenendi Parliamentum: Irish or English' in *England and Ireland in the Later Middle Ages*, ed. J. Lydon (Dublin, 1981), pp. 122−52. The question is far from closed. See the review article by M. Prestwich in *Parliamentary History: a Yearbook*, 1 (1982), 221−5.

6 *Parliamentary Texts*, ed. Pronay and Taylor, p. 90. And see Roskell, 'Consideration of *Modus*', pp. 413−16.

7 See the works noted in the Bibliography by Buck, Denton, Haines, Walsh and Wright.

the training of bishops in universities or in royal government and their later pastoral and political activities. To examine the work of churchmen at the parish level is to move into an area of study where the evidence is much more intractable. Recent research on the beneficed clergy, building upon earlier works notably by A. Hamilton Thompson and J. R. H. Moorman,[8] has sometimes been on a regional basis, as for example the East Riding of Yorkshire or Lincolnshire,[9] and sometimes on a topical basis, as for example the education of the clergy[10] or the changing patterns in the patronage of churches.[11] There remains a pressing need to understand more in general about the rectors, vicars and chaplains of the parishes, their background and training, and their social and political standing. This study relates especially to their political standing. Decisions of the ecclesiastical hierarchy and of kings concerning the Church are often seen as imposed from above. But how far was royal government influenced by the opinions and interests of the army of churchmen whose primary concern, in theory at least, was the cure of souls?

Many of the lower clergy's representatives were, as we shall

---

[8] Thompson, *English Clergy* and Moorman, *Church Life*.

[9] D. Robinson, *Beneficed Clergy in Cleveland and the East Riding 1306–1340* (Borthwick Papers 37, York, 1969) and D. M. Owen, *Church and Society in Medieval Lincolnshire* (Lincoln, 1971). And see B. Mains, 'The Beneficed Clergy of the Diocese of Canterbury 1279–1313' (Oxford D.Phil., 1976), P. H. Hase, 'The Development of the Parish in Hampshire, particularly in the Twelfth and Thirteenth Centuries' (Cambridge Ph.D., 1976) and M. J. Franklin, 'Minsters and Parishes: Northamptonshire Studies' (Cambridge Ph.D., 1982).

[10] See C. J. Godfrey, 'Non-residence of parochial clergy in the fourteenth century', *Church Quarterly Review*, 162 (1961), 433–46; L. E. Boyle, 'The constitution "Cum ex eo" of Boniface VIII', *Medieval Studies*, 24 (1962), 263–302 and R. M. Haines, 'The education of the English clergy during the later middle ages: some observations on the operation of Boniface VIII's constitution "Cum ex eo"', *Canadian Journal of History*, 4 (1969), 1–22.

[11] J. E. Newman, 'Greater and lesser landowners and parochial patronage: Yorkshire in the thirteenth century', *EHR*, 92 (1977), 280–308 and R. K. Rose, 'Priests and patrons in the fourteenth-century diocese of Carlisle' in *The Church in Town and Countryside (Studies in Church History*, 16), ed. D. Baker (Oxford, 1979), pp. 207–18. And see R. Donaldson, 'Patronage and the Church: a study of the social structure of the secular clergy in the diocese of Durham 1311–1540' (Edinburgh Ph.D., 1952) and P. C. Saunders, 'Royal ecclesiastical patronage in England 1199–1351' (Oxford D.Phil., 1978).

see,[12] men who had received training in the universities. We know all too little about the influence of men of learning upon the Crown. The fact that Dominicans had a high place of favour in the king's court is worthy of special note and further investigation.[13] And it is well known that college and university benefactors were often men prominent in royal government.[14] As F. M. Powicke stressed in his presidential address to the Royal Historical Society in 1936, 'the political historian, if he really wishes to understand the development of the state, can no more afford to neglect the glossators and the publicists than he can afford to neglect the charter, the plea roll and the chronicle'.[15] Recently J. R. Maddicott has written of the negotiations between Henry III and the barons in 1264: 'If anything had become more evident during the negotiations, it was the close connection between the practical world of politics and the academic world of the schools, a linkage often noted but rarely so well substantiated.' Simon de Montfort had offered in 1264 'to submit to the arbitration of "bishops and men of religion, knowing the law of God" ("who have read the decretals or have becomingly taught theology and sacred philosophy", according to the Song of Lewes)'.[16] The Crown's links with the learning of churchmen is not an easy area of study to open up. But we know enough to be sure that royal policies and attitudes should not be studied irrespective of developments in the schools. A prime instance is provided by the demands for aid in the defence of the realm and the teaching of the doctrine of necessity.[17] It is thus quite startling to read in the preface to the new analysis of the reign of

---

[12] Below pp. 72—3.

[13] C. F. R. Palmer, 'The king's confessors, 1256—1450', *The Antiquary*, 22 (1890), 114—20, 159—61, 262—6, and 23 (1891), 24—6, W. A. Hinnebusch, *The Early English Friars Preachers* (Rome, 1951), esp. pp. 458—91, and Wright, *Church and Crown*, pp. 232—5.

[14] See now Buck, *Walter Stapeldon*, pp. 100—1.

[15] F. M. Powicke, 'Reflections on the medieval state', *Trans. of the Royal Hist. Soc.*, 4th ser. 19 (1936), 4—5.

[16] J. R. Maddicott, 'The mise of Lewes, 1264', *EHR*, 98 (1983), 591.

[17] See Denton, *Winchelsey*, esp. p. 97 and the references cited there (for 'document', line 7, read 'doctrine'), Post, *Studies*, passim, J. R. Strayer, 'Defense of the realm and royal power in France' in *Studi in Onore di Gino Luzzato* (Milan, 4 vols., 1950), I. 289—96 (reprinted in *Medieval Statecraft and the Perspectives of History*, ed. J. F. Benton and T. N. Bisson (Princeton, 1971), pp. 291—9) and M. Asheri, 'Note per la storia dello stato di necessità: la sistemazione canonistica', *Studi Senesi*, ser.3 vol. 24 (1975), 7—94.

Philip the Fair that the author has not 'discussed political theories or the theological controversies of the learned because they had little influence on events'.[18] The case, for France just as for England, cannot rest there.

Which churchmen, then, were present in parliament? The main groups were the prelates and ecclesiastical dignitaries, individually summoned, and the cathedral chapters and diocesan clergy, summoned to attend by proxy. But these were not all.[19] Some royal clerks, among them 'masters' of Chancery, were summoned to be present with others of the king's council, including royal justices.[20] This was, without question, a very influential group of royal clerks, which contained men about whom we are beginning to know a good deal, for example Peter de Dene and John de Cadamo.[21] Some of this group were cathedral deans or archdeacons, like John de Derby, dean of Lichfield, and Robert de Radewell, archdeacon of Chester. Although the title of 'magister' for the chief clerks of Chancery perhaps became honorific by Edward III's reign,[22] many of these men acting as advisers in parliament, were without doubt university-trained.[23] In addition to summoning royal clerks, Edward I, for the parliament of January 1301 (at which there was discussion concerning Boniface VIII's remarkable bull 'Scimus fili', claiming that the realm of Scotland belonged *pleno iure* to the Roman Church), took the unusual step of summoning legal experts from the universities of Oxford and Cambridge, four or five from Oxford and two or three from

---

18 J. R. Strayer, *The Reign of Philip the Fair* (Princeton, 1980), p. xiii. For a quite different approach to the politics of the age see J. N. Hillgarth, *Ramon Lull and Lullism in Fourteenth-Century France* (Oxford, 1971) pp. 46−134.

19 See Denton, 'Clergy and parliament', pp. 88−9.

20 See, for example, those summoned to the parliaments of Sept. 1297 (*Parl. Writs*, I. ii. 55), March 1300 (I. ii. 83), July 1302 (I. ii. 113), Feb. 1309 (II. ii. 24) and Aug. 1312 (II. ii. 73). And see H. G. Richardson and G. Sayles, 'The king's ministers in parliament 1272−1377', *EHR*, 46 (1931), 529−50 and 47 (1932), 194−203, 377−97.

21 Denton, *Winchelsey*, pp. 281−3, 292−4 and Cheney, *Notaries*, pp. 143−51. And see Cheney, 'Law and letters in fourteenth-century Durham', p. 85.

22 T. F. Tout, *Chapters in the Administrative History of Medieval England* (Manchester, 1920−33), III. 211 and Cheney, *Notaries*, p. 89.

23 See, for example, Peter de Dene, Robert de Radewell, John de Craucumbe, William de Grenefeld, William de Kilkenny and John de Lacy in Emden, *Oxford*.

Cambridge.[24] On other occasions the king and his government may well have been influenced by churchmen, secular clerks or monks, who were present at times of parliament though not formally summoned. Individual petitions were presented by, or on behalf of, churchmen and churches of all kinds at times of parliament.[25] The warden of Merton College, Oxford, and two fellows of the college, spent four weeks at the parliament ('in parliamento') held at London in March 1300.[26] And, as a further indication of the danger of assuming that only the summoned clergy were present at times of parliament, twelve abbots who were not summoned certainly sent their proctors to the parliament of Carlisle in 1307, perhaps because of a special interest in the king's statute which forbade the payment of dues by monasteries to Orders or parent-houses abroad.[27] These are reminders that churchmen, in diverse ways, were involved with, as well as in, royal government — and times of parliament were no exception. Clerks and laymen worked together at each level of government.

Yet, there is no doubt that changes of far-reaching significance in the political and social interrelations of clergy and laity were taking place in Western Europe around the turn of the thirteenth century. Many aspects of these changes remain to be explored, in the realms both of political ideas and of political activity — from the world of papal and royal courts and the world of the learned to the linked world of the parish clergy. The implication of much that has been written on the English parliament as it developed in the late thirteenth and early fourteenth centuries is that the authority and influence of the laity increased at the expense of the authority and influence of the clergy. The notion of the 'community of the realm' developed into the constitutionalised lay commons. The emergence of a commons of laymen during this period, at the heart of government and associating the localities with the centre, is beyond dispute. But the reasons for the growth of a specifically lay commons, and the emphasis we should give, especially during the reigns of Edward I and Edward II, to this embryonic institution of government, are still open to debate. The debate must take into account the continuing political involvement of the Church and the clergy.

---

[24] *Parl. Writs*, I. ii. 91. Oxford sent four legal experts and Cambridge two: see W. Prynne, *The Third Tome of Our Exact Chronological Vindication* . . . (London, 1668, reissued 1670, 1672), pp. 884—5.

[25] Denton, 'Clergy and Parliament', pp. 97—9.

[26] *Early Rolls of Merton*, ed. Highfield, pp. 338—9, 341—2.

[27] Denton, 'Clergy and parliament', p. 90 n. 7.

The names of all the known proctors of the lower clergy are listed in Appendix 5 and are included in the General Index, and there is a brief discussion of the kind of men elected by the clergy in Chapter 5.[28] This information, concerning a total of 199 proctors for cathedral chapters and 124 for diocesan clergy, will be of some importance for further work on the beneficed clergy and on the composition of cathedral chapters. But the omission from this study of biographical material concerning all the proctors is deliberate. In the first place, the searching of published evidence, especially bishops' registers, produces in general only scraps of miscellaneous information. Secondly, the extant sources have provided us only rarely with the names of proctors for a sequence of parliaments from a given 'constituency', and this is especially true of the proctors of the diocesan clergy. Only for the three northern dioceses do names of diocesan proctors survive for more than a very few parliaments (York diocese: twenty-four proctors, five of whom were elected more than once, for fifteen parliaments; Carlisle diocese: seventeen proctors, four elected more than once, for eleven parliaments; and Durham diocese: seventeen proctors, two elected more than once, for eleven parliaments). For the southern dioceses, more proctors are known for Worcester and for Winchester than for other dioceses: respectively, seven proctors for five parliaments and seven proctors for four parliaments. For one parliament, the Carlisle parliament of 1307, we do have enough names (thirty-five from the dioceses and twenty-six from the cathedral chapters) to provide data for a prosopographical study, based upon their grouping in parliament. But such an analysis would require more evidence of the position of these elected clerks in their dioceses or chapters, in relation to other churchmen, than is in fact available.

Some other limits of this study need to be stressed. We have not brought into the discussion the proctors of individual churchmen. A distinction was drawn in the *Modus* between the 'higher' clergy, summoned to parliament by reason of tenure, and the 'lesser' clergy, who were not legally bound to attend parliament.[29] The latter were the archdeacons, deans or priors and chapters of cathedral churches, and the diocesan clergy. Of these 'lesser' clergy we have concerned ourselves only with the elected representatives of the cathedral chapters (one summoned from each chapter) and of

[28] Below pp. 72—5.
[29] *Parl. Texts*, ed. Pronay and Taylor, p. 68. And see Denton, 'Clergy and parliament', pp. 89—92.

8

the diocesan clergy (two summoned from each diocese). All other churchmen — bishops, abbots, archdeacons, priors or deans of cathedral churches — were summoned to parliament as individuals. And in bringing together the two kinds of elected proctors, representing groups of clergy, there is no intention to imply that they necessarily viewed themselves as very closely associated. While the proctors of the diocesan or parish clergy (on occasion referred to specifically as the 'communitas cleri') may well have often formed a distinct group in both parliaments and ecclesiastical councils, as they did in 1296 and 1297,[30] the proctors of the cathedral chapters probably aligned themselves with the middle ranks of the clergy, with the ecclesiastical dignitaries, the deans and the archdeacons, or, where the cathedral church was monastic, with the religious.[31] Both the proctors of dioceses and the proctors of chapters were, however, fully representatives, for there can be no suspicion that they merely presented excuses for the absence of those summoned.[32]

Also, we have distinguished the ecclesiastical assemblies in parliament from those outside parliament, that is parliaments from ecclesiastical councils or convocations. In some practical respects it makes little sense to distinguish between the different assemblies in which the clergy met;[33] and it is especially noteworthy that the clergy were often summoned in these years to meet in parliament not only by royal writs but also by writs from the archbishops of Canterbury or York.[34] Yet, whether or not the clergy should be drawn into parliament — a secular court — and by what kind of summons were important issues of the time, and there was debate on these matters precisely because the clergy themselves were concerned about the fundamental legal distinction between a summons to appear before the king and a summons to appear before the archbishop. If letters of proxy from the lower clergy had survived in

[30] See Clarke, *Representation*, pp. 321–3.
[31] The proctors of the subprior and chapter of Rochester for the parliament of March 1313 were given power to act 'una cum aliis procuratoribus religiosorum' (PRO SC10/2/100: see Appendix 1(d)), whereas the dean and chapter of Bangor, for the same parliament, promised to accept whatever was done by their proctor 'ex unanimi consensu decanorum et procuratorum capitulorum regni Anglie' (SC10/2/93).
[32] Exceptionally the York clergy sent proxies in 1339–41 which did just this: see below pp. 52.
[33] Denton, 'Clergy and parliament', pp. 94–5.
[34] See below pp. 19–22.

large numbers for ecclesiastical councils, it would have been essential to study them alongside the letters for parliaments. But it appears that none at all are extant, as originals or as enregistered copies, from the diocesan clergy for ecclesiastical councils,[35] and the number of survivals from the capitular clergy for ecclesiastical councils is much less — and only as enregistered copies — than for parliaments.

To begin in 1295, when all ranks of the clergy were first summoned to parliament along with all ranks of the laity, is not to ignore the fact that capitular and diocesan clergy had been summoned to attend earlier assemblies.[36] At least three of these earlier assemblies can be firmly regarded as summoned by royal authority: the council or parliament of April 1254, which included capitular and diocesan clergy, summoned by the king's regents; the ecclesiastical council at Northampton (and at York for the northern province) of January 1283, which included capitular clergy, summoned at the instance of the king to appear before the king or his deputies; and the ecclesiastical council of September 1294, which included capitular and diocesan clergy, summoned by the king to treat with the king.[37] Nonetheless, the so-called Model parliament of 1295 was of especially wide composition and marks the first occasion of the use of the 'premunientes' clause (in the writs addressed to each bishop), which became the standard means for the summoning of the lower clergy to parliament. From early in Edward II's reign the 'premunientes' clause was often supplemented by separate archiepiscopal writs. The year 1340, or more precisely the parliament of 29 March 1340, is a conveninent *terminus ad*

---

[35] As a result, we only rarely, and from other evidence, know the names of the proctors of diocesan clergy attending ecclesiastical councils: see *Reg. Grandisson*, p. 766, and below p. 18. n. 1. A rare proxy, for a later ecclesiastical council, appears in *John Lydford's Book*, ed. D. M. Owen (HMSO, and Devon and Cornwall Record Soc. 19, 1974), no. 23: appointment by the clergy of the archdeaconry of Surrey of John Lydford, official of Winchester, as their proctor in the council to be held at St Paul's London on 9 May 1379. And for a memorandum of the election of the proctors of the clergy of the diocese of Ely for the ecclesiastical council of 9 Nov. 1377 see Aston, *Arundel*, p. 409.

[36] See Clarke, *Representation*, pp. 296–312 and Denton, 'Clergy and parliament', pp. 96–7. It was probably because of the archiepiscopal vacancy that the dean and chapter of York had been summoned to a parliament in 1265 (ibid., p. 96 n. 21).

[37] Sayles, *King's Parliament*, p. 44 and *Councils and Synods II*, pp. 481–3, 939–44, 1125–7.

quem, because this marks the last occasion on which the king's writs to the bishops were reinforced by archiepiscopal writs.[38] No immediate effects upon the actual attendance of lower clergy in parliament can be demonstrated. Indeed, some lower clergy continued to attend parliaments throughout the century and beyond.[39] After 1340 there was, even so, a more distinct separation, practical as well as legal, between parliament and the convocations of Canterbury and York. From this time there could be no reversing the trend whereby the clergy *qua* clergy exercised their political influence in the main through convocations; and, by significant contrast, the crisis of 1340 provided the first unmistakable demonstration that the lay commons in parliament had emerged as an independent and co-ordinated political force.[40]

At the centre of this study is the evidence provided by the letters which granted the power to act to the clergy's representatives. These proctorial letters are sometimes termed 'mandates' or 'warrants'. Here we have usually preferred 'letters of proxy' or simply 'proxies'. A large number form classification SC10 (Parliamentary Proxies) in the Public Record Office.[41] Until recently these files of clerical proxies have attracted little attention.[42] The whole group for the parliament of February 1324 had appeared in Palgrave's *Parliamentary Writs* of 1827−34, and a collection from the bishop and clergy of Carlisle had been printed in 1913 as an appendix to the edition of Bishop Halton's register.[43] Yet, Maude Clarke, whose extremely valuable work on the lower clergy in *Medieval Representation and Consent* (1936) was based upon a close investigation of

---

[38] Below pp. 19−21.

[39] See McHardy, 'Representation of clergy', esp. p. 107.

[40] Harriss, *King, Parliament and Finance*, p. 259.

[41] This classification was formed, it seems, in the late 1880s: *The Fiftieth Report of the Deputy Keeper of the Public Records* (London, 1889), p. x. One group of 26 ecclesiastical proxies, for the parliament of Sept. 1334, is a separate file among the Writs and Returns of Members to Parliament (PRO C219/5/17); and a proxy of the archdeaconry of Salop for the parliament of 1309 is among the Chancery Ecclesiastical Miscellanea (C270/35/17). See Appendices 1 and 5. (A group of proxies from abbots for the parliament or council of 23 Sept. 1353 is among Chancery Parliament and Council Proceedings, C49/46/28−41, /47/1, as noted by H. G. Richardson and G. Sayles, 'The parliaments of Edward III', *BIHR*, 8 (1930−1), 70 n. 7.)

[42] See esp. Roskell, 'Problem of attendance', *idem*, 'Consideration of *Modus*' and McHardy, 'Representation of clergy'.

[43] *Parl. Writs*, II. ii. 294−9 and *Reg. Halton*, II. 231−5.

the sources, was apparently unaware of the survival of these proxies.[44] Well over 1100 clerical proxies survive in the Public Record Office for the period under discussion here, and many more were copied into ecclesiastical registers, notably the registers of bishops and cathedral priors. The great majority were for proctors representing absent individual prelates and ecclesiastical dignitaries. Of those which name the proctors of diocesan and cathedral clergy we have collected 221 full proxies, 181 of which are originals in the Public Record Office.[45]

Clearly these proxies are a major source of information concerning the representation of the clergy in parliament. But since discussion of parliamentary representation has hitherto concentrated upon the laity, we must consider briefly the procedures whereby the shires and boroughs sent their nominees to parliament. It became, during the reign of Edward I, the usual practice for each sheriff to act as the returning officer both for the shire court and the borough courts within his county.[46] After elections in the county court and in the borough courts, the writ of summons was returned by the sheriff, with the names of the elected men entered on the dorse of the writ or on an added schedule.[47] Lay electoral procedures were regularised by legislation in the late fourteenth and early fifteenth centuries, and by the statute of 1406 the results of elections were required to be returned by indentures sealed by the electors.[48] Usually included in these indentures was a specific statement —

---

[44] Thus, she suggested in error that the southern clergy did not attend the parliaments at York in 1319 and Feb. 1328, nor any northern parliament thereafter, and that northern clerical proctors did not attend parliaments south of the Trent after 1327: Clarke, *Representation*, pp. 144–6.

[45] See Appendix 5.

[46] For the parliament of May 1306 the sheriffs were also ordered to inform all the prelates and religious in their shires that they should appear in person or by proxy. This was in addition to the direct summons of bishops and abbots. *Parl. Writs*, I. ii. 164.

[47] See J. S. Roskell, *The Commons in the Parliament of 1422* (Manchester, 1954), 1–37, McKisack, *Representation of Boroughs*, pp. 1–43, Maddicott, 'Parliament and constituencies', pp. 72–8, G. Lapsley, 'Knights of the shire in the parliaments of Edward II', *EHR*, 34 (1919), 25–42, 152–71 (reprinted in *Crown, Community and Parliament* (Oxford, 1951)), and J. S. Illsley, 'Parliamentary elections in the reign of Edward I', *BIHR*, 49 (1976), 24–40.

[48] For indentures in print see *Brief Register*, ed. Prynne, II. 128–32, III. 152–7, 161–3, 168, 171, 173–7, 252–312 and McKisack, *Representation of Boroughs*, pp. 158–60.

reiterating the terms of the writ of summons — of the 'full power' granted to the representatives. The indentures were a late development. Previously the Crown obtained assurance of the authority of the lay representatives from the writs returned by the sheriffs, even though these very often did no more than add to the returned summons the names of the elected men.

Were there, then, no letters of proxy sent by the lay communities? In respect of the counties, this certainly appears to have been the case. Only on one occasion, it seems — for an assembly of April 1268 — did a summons specify that the representatives should come to the king supplied with letters patent declaring their powers of representation: 'cum vestris patentibus sigillo communitatis vestre signatis sub forma quam vobis mittimus presentibus interclusa'. The common form of the letters patent suggested by the Crown on this occasion included the all-important *ratihabitio* clause: 'et nos quicquid ipsi in premissis nomine nostro fecerint ratum habebimus et acceptum'.[49] This summons of 1268 was sent directly to twenty-seven selected cities and boroughs, and their representatives presumably came to the assembly, as instructed, with their letters patent. Now, the *Modus* stated that the proctors of the clergy, the representatives from the Cinque Ports, the knights of the shire, the citizens and burgesses all came to parliament with their warrants.[50] And it was, indeed, by this time to be expected that anyone commissioned to exercise any kind of proctorial authority, in whatever court, would need his letters of proxy specifying his powers. But not, it seems, the knights of the shire in parliament. The fact that many of the returned writs bore a statement of the 'full power' granted to the named representatives itself suggests that the return of the writs of summons, with endorsements or added schedules, took the place of warrants.[51] And, whereas the list of proctors of the clergy for the Carlisle parliament of 1307 was drawn up from the letters of proxy, the list of knights of the shire and of burgesses was drawn up from the sheriffs' returned writs.[52] Perhaps this reliance upon the sheriffs' returned writs is not without some significance. It cannot be explained away simply by stating that the county courts possessed

---

[49] Sayles, 'Representation of cities and boroughs', p. 585, and see below p. 38.

[50] *Parl. Texts*, ed. Pronay and Taylor, pp. 68−70, and concerning duplicates see below pp. 35−6.

[51] See the printed returns in *Parl. Writs*, I. ii and II. ii.

[52] *Parl. Writs*, I. ii. 184−90.

no seals, for documents drawn up on behalf of the communities of the shires could have been authenticated by the seals of others.[53] While there is no denying the capacity of the knights and land-owners of the shires to act corporately and independently through the shire courts, and themselves to empower their proctors, the rôle of the sheriff in the electing of representatives and the sending of them to parliament was clearly of crucial importance.[54]

Gaines Post believed that no letters of proxy from the shires or cities and boroughs survive: 'Unfortunately the actual mandates brought with the returned writs do not survive.'[55] As we have seen, it is probable that there never were any for the shires. Some do, however, survive from the boroughs — though it is unlikely that they were normally brought to parliament with the returned writs. It is surprising that they were not examined by May McKisack in her work on borough representation in parliament. London stands apart, for it was summoned directly; and for London the writ was returned with an endorsement and a letter of proxy was drawn up.[56] Other surviving proxies come from cities of importance, notably Bristol, Ipswich and Southampton.[57] Where a sheriff's return survives as well as a borough proxy, the latter frequently either provides the names missing from the return or it names proc-tors different from those on the return. Although proxies were on occasion simply additional to the returned writ, it thus appears that they sometimes provided names which had not been sent to the sheriff in time and they sometimes corrected the names first sent to

---

[53] See below p. 35 n. 68.
[54] See Maddicott, 'Parliament and constituencies', pp. 72—4.
[55] Post, '*Plena potestas* and consent', p. 153 n. 197.
[56] See *Parl. Writs*, I. ii. 85, 146, II. ii. 7, 30, 78, 129, 144, 204, 252, 270, 339, and PRO C219/5/3/14 (proxy for parl. of Feb. 1328) and C219/5/15/11 (for Feb. 1334).
[57] For the period up to 1340: proxy from Scarborough for Oct. 1307 (C219/2/1/10); from Bristol for Jan. 1316 (C219/3/5a/1); from Yarmouth for Jan. 1316 (C219/3/5a/2); from Lincoln for May 1322 (C219/4/1/14, in *Parl. Writs*, II. ii. 252 & *Return of Members*, p. 65n); from Ipswich for Sept. 1327 (C219/5/1/15); from Southampton for Sept. 1327 (C219/5/1/25, in *Brief Register*, ed. Prynne, III. 287); from Bristol for Apr. 1328 (*ibid.*, 355); from Ipswich for Apr. 1328 (C219/5/4/16); from Bristol for Nov. 1330 (SC10/14/687, misfiled); from Southampton for Mar. 1332 (C219/5/11/27); and from Norwich for May 1335 (C219/5/18/17). For some later borough proxies see *Brief Register*, ed. Prynne, III. 274, 284—5, 356 and E. Gillett, *A History of Grimsby* (London, 1970), p. 304.

14

the sheriff.[58] They were probably brought to parliament by the proctors themselves. Unusually, Ipswich in 1327 returned directly to the Crown the writ from the sheriff (which included the royal writ) and added its endorsement naming two representatives, and, in addition, sent a letter of proxy;[59] and, unusually also by this date, in 1337 boroughs were sent a separate royal summons, and they responded by acting like the sheriffs, returning the royal writs with endorsements.[60]

Study of both the returns and the proxies demands the greatest care. It must be understood, for example, that the survival of a returned writ is no proof that the named shire and borough representatives actually attended the parliament in question. The returns for the parliament of May 1298 illustrate the point. Clearly they had been sent in advance of the expected arrival of the nominees, for, although there is no indication to this effect in the printed list of *Return of Members*,[61] the comment that no representatives appeared ('Non ven'', 'Nullus ven'' or 'Non ven' aliquis') has been written on the dorse of ten of the writs. And we learn, too, that only a few representatives appeared from several other counties.[62] The addition to the writs of these brief notes alerts us to the fact that there was a very low attendance of lay representatives at this York parliament of 1298, only about half of those named in the returns. But the survival in the Public Record Office of proxies from the boroughs or the clergy, as well as, indeed, from absent individuals, is, in each individual case, a surer indication of proctorial attendance, for who can have brought the proxies to parliament other than the named proctors, or at least one of the named proctors?

But the proxies present many problems of their own. In examining all those from the lower clergy we have been fully aware of a danger succinctly expressed by J. G. Edwards: 'In the deserts of common form the unwary traveller may easily be duped by a verbal mirage.'[63] Of course, the proxies do have features in common. Successions of them from some dioceses are very similar.

---

[58] There is, also, a reference to a proxy from Scarborough for the Carlisle parliament of 1307, which apparently amended the sheriff's return (*Parl. Writs*, I. ii. 190 and *Return of Members*, I. 26).

[59] PRO C219/5/1/14 and /15.

[60] *Return of Members*, pp. 113 (C219/6/2), 115 (C219/6/5).

[61] *Return of Members*, pp. 8—10.

[62] See *Parl. Writs*, I. ii. 65—77.

[63] Edwards, 'Personnel of the Commons', p. 210.

Occasionally, indeed, there are a few identical in form.[64] Yet, within certain bounds, the overall diversity of terminology is striking, and instructive. A detailed analysis is possible precisely because so many have survived. An initial comparison of the clerical proxies with the few borough proxies suggests no great differences, but clerical representation had in fact distinctive features, some of which are apparent in the proxies. Certainly, we can learn much more from them than just the names of the proctors. They will assist us, along with other evidence especially from bishops' registers, to an understanding of the practicalities of election, attendance and representation. Above all, they bring us nearer than any other evidence to a comprehension of the actual powers granted to the representatives, to the realities, in fact, of 'full power'.[65] J. G. Edwards argued that one of the roots of the legal sovereignty of parliament was the 'full power' of the representatives of the commons, and he sought to strengthen his argument by noting the use of the term *attornati* for some of the borough representatives of the fourteenth century, for power of attorney implied plenipotentiary power.[66] But, while it is obviously the case that the legal sovereignty of parliament developed in due course of time out of the power of the representatives to act as representatives, it is quite misguided, as Post realised, to suggest that the granting of 'full power' implied anything more than the acceptance in advance of decisions to be reached in common counsel.[67] It was essentially a limiting rather than an unlimited power. It was a submission to royal authority, though not one which prevented the possibility of debate and discussion. And, as the clerical proxies demonstrate, it was a submission which the clergy were not always willing to make. Post commented that he had found little evidence of 'limited' mandates being drawn up for parliament,[68] mandates, that is, that did not grant full power to give consent. The clerical proxies provide some examples, for the clergy were eager to defend a status which protected them from the full rigours of royal authority. Even so, it is certain that our individual agents were not bearers of a particular authority which actually derogated

---

[64] For example, from York clergy SC10/6/255 (see Appendix 1(f)), /6/276, /7/336 & /7/349, and from clergy of Durham archdeaconry SC10/18/870 and /19/944 (see Appendix 1(k)).

[65] For the *plena potestas* of clerical representatives before 1295 see Denton, 'Clergy and parliament', pp. 95–7.

[66] Edwards, *'Plena potestas'*, pp. 153–4.

[67] See esp. Post, *'Plena potestas* and consent', pp. 91, 161.

[68] *Ibid.*, p. 153.

in any legal or constitutional way from the authority of the Crown. As for *attornatus*, it is doubtful whether this was to be distinguished at the time from the term *procurator*, although the one was associated with the royal courts and the other with the ecclesiastical courts. The drafters of the clerical proxies employed both, and we could just as well use the term 'attorneys' for the clerical representatives as for the lay representatives.[69] However, the proxies more frequently refer to *procuratores*, and, rather than treating terms with different associations as synonyms, we shall avoid 'attorneys' in favour of 'proctors'.

[69] And see *Select Cases in the Court of King's Bench*, ed. G. O. Sayles, I (Selden Soc., 55, 1936), p. xci.

2

Summons and Election

The drawing-up of the letters of proxy for the clerical representatives was the final stage in an electoral procedure which was initiated by writs of summons. The sheriffs, as we have noted, acted as the returning officers for both the knights of the shires and the borough representatives. But the bishops were not in the same relationship to the Crown in respect of the clerical representatives, for the lower clergy were 'forewarned' — not ordered — to be present. Royal writs to bishops did not include the final legal requirement 'et habeas ibi hoc breve'. In these circumstances the clerical letters of proxy brought to parliament must have assumed a special significance. When the clergy were summoned only by royal writs, the proxies were, by the nature of things, the only authentication of the proctors' authority to act.

Yet, when the bishops were in receipt of an archiepiscopal writ ordering them to summon the clergy of their dioceses they then acted as returning officers to the archbishops for the clerical representatives, as did the sheriffs to the king for the lay representatives. Each bishop was instructed to present the archbishop with a certificate of execution citing the terms of the writ of summons. In a similar way to the sheriffs' returns, a schedule was attached to the certificate of execution, which gave a list of those summoned. But these schedules did not always — as the surviving enregistered copies show — give the actual names of the representatives who had been elected.[1] The issuing of proxies was additional to, and separate from, the bishop's certificate of execution with its attached schedule. When there was a provincial writ for a parliament it is

---

[1] For examples see *Councils and Synods II*, pp. 1301—2, 1325—7, 1363, *Reg. Grandisson*, pp. 446—8 (*Concilia*, II. 548—9), *Reg. Martival*, II. i. 98, II. ii. 530, 543—4, *Reg. Halton*, II. 119, 180, CRO, Reg. Kirkby, pp. 328, 366, HWRO, Reg. Montacute, pp. 144—5, 172 and CUL, EDR, Reg. Montacute, fo. 38v.

not certain that all bishops responded to both the archbishop's writ and the king's writ for the same parliament. But, in addition to entries in episcopal registers, the proxies themselves show that the archbishops' provincial writs were being frequently executed, indeed perhaps regularly executed.[2]

The provincial writs of summons of the lower clergy to parliament, described by Clarke as 'nothing more than a whip issued to secure full attendance of the clergy for purposes of taxation',[3] require further explanation. They are important for an understanding of the first stage in the process leading to the election of representatives. The provincial writ issued by the archbishops, consequent upon a royal mandate to both archbishops, was always, after 1311, supplementary to the royal writ with the 'premunientes' clause sent to each bishop. There had been one earlier attempt, in 1283, by the Crown to summon the clergy, through the archbishops of Canterbury and York, by the use of enforceable writs ('venire faciatis'),[4] but the ordering of provincial writs specifically for parliaments began in 1311 (for 18 November revised to 2 December, a late session of the parliament which began in August) and was the frequent practice until the parliament of March 1340. Between 1311 and 1340 there was a total of thirty-seven parliaments to which the lower clergy were summoned and for twenty-four of these parliaments we have a record of the king's order that provincial writs be issued by his archbishops.[5] As we

---

[2] For the registers see *Reg. Martival*, II. i. 345−7, II. ii. 435−7 and other refs. below n. 5; and for the proxies see below pp. 23−4.

[3] Clarke, *Representation*, p. 133. The recent editors of the *Modus* appear to have assumed that the statement there concerning two kinds of summons for the clergy was a reference to the summons of the lower clergy by the writ including the 'premunientes' clause and by the provincial writ (*Parliamentary Texts*, ed. Pronay and Taylor, pp. 23, 68); but the two kinds of summons which the author of the *Modus* had in mind were clearly the summons, on the one hand, of the higher clergy by reason of tenure and, on the other hand, of the lower clergy who could be asked, but not required, to attend.

[4] *Councils and Synods II*, p. 941.

[5] For a survey of some of the evidence concerning the summoning of the clergy to parliament between 1311 and 1340 see Kemp, *Counsel and Consent*, pp. 91−106. The 24 parliaments for which a provincial writ was ordered by the king were as follows:

   1311 Dec.: *Parl. Writs*, II. ii. 57−8 and Wake, *State of the Church*, app. p. 34; and see Clarke, *Representation*, pp. 130−1 and Denton, *Winchelsey*, p. 265 n. 348.

   1314 Sept.: *Parl. Writs*, II. ii. 128, and see Denton, 'Reynolds and

shall see, the nature of the royal mandate changed, and, in addition, the archbishops did not always respond in the same way.

Archbishop Winchelsey took exception to the terms of the royal mandate for the parliament of 1311, but it is not clear exactly which terms he found objectionable. He may well have disliked the new procedure of being ordered to issue provincial writs, but in fact, on

---

ecclesiastical politics', p. 259 n. 61.

1315 Jan.: *Parl. Writs*, II. ii. 138, and see Denton, 'Reynolds and ecclesiastical politics', p. 259 n. 61.

1316 Jan.: *Parl. Writs*, II. ii. 154, and see Denton, 'Reynolds and ecclesiastical politics', p. 262 nn. 75–6.

1321 July: *Parl. Writs*, II. ii. 236, LPL, Reg. Reynolds, fo. 299, Norwich, D. & C. Muniments, Reg. IX, fo. 30v (*Concilia*, II. 506–7), Worcester, D. & C. Muniments, Liber Albus, fo. 101r (*Liber Albus*, ed. Wilson, p. 71), and *Reg. Martival*, II. i. 345–7.

1322 May: *Parl. Writs*, II. ii. 247, LPL, Reg. Reynolds, fo. 304r and *Reg. Martival*, II. ii. 388–9.

1324 Feb.: *Parl. Writs*, II. ii. 292, Wake, *State of the Church*, app. pp. 51–3, *Reg. Orleton*, pp. 273–5 and *Reg. Martival*, II. ii. 435.

1327 Jan.: *Parl. Writs*, II. ii. 353 and *Reg. Martival*, II. ii. 530–1.

1327 Sept.: *Dignity of a Peer*, IV. 378 and *Reg. Martival*, II. ii. 540–1.

1328 Feb.: *Dignity of a Peer*, IV. 380 and *Reg. Martival*, II. ii. 553–4.

1328 July: *Dignity of a Peer*, IV. 386 and *Concilia*, II. 545–6.

1328 Oct.: *Dignity of a Peer*, IV. 389 and *Reg. Martival*, II. ii. 578–9.

1330 March: *Dignity of a Peer*, IV. 394, *Concilia*, II. 557, SRO, Reg. Shrewsbury, fo. 17v (calendered in *Reg. Shrewsbury*, pp. 32–3) and LRO, Reg. Northburgh, fo. 107.

1332 March: *Dignity of a Peer*, IV. 411.

1334 Feb.: *Dignity of a Peer*, IV. 425 and *Concilia*, II. 570.

1334 Sept.: *Dignity of a Peer*, IV. 430 and HWRO, Reg. Montacute, p. 143.

1335 May: *Dignity of a Peer*, IV. 446.

1336 March: *Dignity of a Peer*, IV. 456 and *Concilia*, II. 581.

1336 Sept.: *Dignity of a Peer*, IV. 463 and CRO, Reg. Kirkby, p. 335.

1337 March: *Dignity of a Peer*, IV. 467, 473.

1339 Feb.: *Dignity of a Peer*, IV. 500, 503 and *Reg. Shrewsbury*, pp. 345–6.

1339 Oct.: *Dignity of a Peer*, IV. 506.

1340 Jan.: *Dignity of a Peer*, IV. 509 and CRO, Reg. Kirkby, pp. 400–2.

1340 March: *Dignity of a Peer*, IV. 518.

this first occasion of its use, the king's order was only for the archbishop to give his authority to the 'forewarning' of the clergy. The position changed after Winchelsey's death. In 1314 Archbishop Reynolds and Archbishop Greenfield of York were ordered to summon separate ecclesiastical assemblies and the orders used the peremptory 'venire faciatis' clause, as in 1283.[6] And later in the year this peremptory clause was used for the first time in writs summoning the clergy to parliament. For the parliament of September 1314, and then for the parliaments of January 1315 and January 1316, the royal writ ordering provincial citations took the form 'mandamus rogantes quatinus venire faciatis'. The offence to clerical privilege was abundantly clear: the archbishops were being required to use their authority to summon the clergy to meet in a secular court. For the parliament of January 1316 the archbishop of Canterbury tried to appease the clergy by convoking them to meet before himself (rather than before the king) on 26 January 'as though at the doors of parliament', which had been summoned for the following day.[7]

For the parliaments of October 1318 and May 1319 the clergy were summoned only by the 'premunientes' writ, but the 'venire faciatis' provincial order re-emerged for the parliaments of July 1321 and May 1322: 'Nos nolentes negotia nostra in dicto parliamento tractanda propter absentiam dictorum decanorum *etc* retardari, vobis mandamus rogantes quatinus . . . venire faciatis.' At least on the first of these occasions, some bishops were reluctant to certify to the execution of the archbishop's writ, and the bishop of Salisbury refused 'eo quod mandatum predictum preiudiciale ut premittitur videbatur'.[8] The archbishop of Canterbury again acted on a peremptory royal order for the parliament of February 1324 ('committimus et mandamus quatinus . . . iniungi faciatis'). But this was the last occasion on which the Crown tried to secure the presence of the clergy by writs which, by their terms, were legally enforceable. A new form of royal provincial order was used for January 1327 and on sixteen occasions during the next thirteen years: 'Nolentes tamen negotia nostra predicta pro defectu premunitionum predictorum, si forsan minus rite facta fuerint, aliqualiter retardari, vobis mandamus firmiter iniungentes (*from March 1332*: mandamus rogantes) quod *premuniri* faciatis.' Thus, there was no longer any direct infringement of clerical rights, and

---

6 Denton, 'Reynolds and ecclesiastical politics', p. 257.
7 Ibid., p. 263 (correct 24 to 26 Jan.).
8 *Reg. Martival*, II. i. 347.

the archbishops during these early years of the reign of Edward III were simply being required, as Winchelsey had been in 1311, to give their authority to the 'premunientes' summons.[9]

Other developments took place in the 1330s which must be briefly noted. The difficulty of ensuring, or of attempting to ensure, that the clergy worked in harmony with parliament was proving to be a major constitutional problem. Already in 1324 a convocation of clergy had been summoned, at the king's order, to meet at St Paul's on the same day, 20 January, as a full parliament was to meet at Westminster; but these citations had been revoked in favour of a parliament, to which the clergy were summoned by the double process, to meet on 23 February.[10] In 1330 the king summoned the clergy to a parliament at Winchester on 11 March by the double process. In response to the provincial order, Archbishop Mepham ordered the Canterbury clergy to assemble on 11 March but before himself rather than before the king. So, if we are to take this distinction seriously, as we surely must, the clergy were summoned to convocation by the archbishop on the same day and in the same city as they were summoned to parliament by the king using the 'premunientes' writ.[11] The *Handbook of British Chronology* thus has a parliament and a convocation meeting on 11 March at Winchester. The one assembly was preparatory to the other, for the archbishop summoned the clergy to treat before himself in the cathedral church 'super negotiis in parliamento predicto diffusius pertractandis'.

In 1334 the king ordered the summoning of a convocation of clergy, and he also summoned the clergy to parliament (to meet on 19 September) by both the 'premunientes' and the provincial writs; Archbishop Stratford responded by citing the clergy to appear before himself at St Paul's, and on the same day as the opening of

---

[9] There is relatively little evidence concerning the execution of provincial writs in the northern province. On occasion there was certainly obstruction. Following the writs for the parliament at Lincoln in Sept. 1327 some of the northern clergy claimed that they were not bound to attend and ought not to be answerable outside their own province, and Archbishop Melton obtained permission from the king and his council to hold a separate provincial council. See Clarke, *Representation*, p. 145.

[10] *Parl. Writs*, II. ii. 288, 291, *Concilia*, II. 519–20, *Reg. Orleton*, pp. 269–71, 273–5, *Reg. Martival*, II. ii. 433, 435–7 and Lincoln, D. & C. Archives, A/2/23, fo. 2.

[11] *Dignity of a Peer*, IV. 391–4, *Concilia*, II. 557–8, *Reg. Shrewsbury*, pp. 29, 32–3, *Reg. Martival*, II. ii. 641–2 and LRO, Reg. Northburgh, fo. 107.

parliament, to discuss the urgent business to be dealt with at greater length in the parliament and to reconvene a week later again before himself and again at St Paul's.[12] Similarly, in the spring of 1336, the archbishop's response, to the provincial order for parliament as in 1330, was to summon a convocation on the same day as parliament before himself and at St Paul's.[13] In the autumn, the king appears to have reacted to these developments, attempting once again to ensure the attendance of the lower clergy in parliament itself but at the same time accepting the desire for a separate convocation of clergy: he ordered the clergy — by the double process — to a parliament at Nottingham and also requested that the clergy should assemble at Leicester a week later.[14] In the autumn of the following year, 1337, only the 'premunientes' writ was used for the parliament at Westminster, but the king also requested a convocation to be summoned to meet four days later at St Paul's. And in 1338 the procedure was similar but much less urgent: at the summer parliament at Northampton the king requested the summoning of a convocation to meet in the autumn.[15] Although the summoning of the lower clergy to parliament was certainly not being abandoned, the convoking of the clergy at the king's instigation but not by direct royal order to separate assemblies, clearly intended to work in cooperation with parliament, was becoming a regular procedure.

Thus, the lower clergy were electing proctors for parliament in response to two kinds of summons: the writ with the 'premunientes' clause was always sent to each bishop, or to the keeper of the spiritualities during a vacancy; and often it was reinforced by a writ from the archbishop. The response to the summons could always be to the king, but might often be to the archbishop. More than two thirds of the surviving letters of proxy from the lower clergy for this period were openly addressed, and most of the rest were addressed to the king. None of those from the province of

[12] *Dignity of a Peer*, IV. 427−30, *Concilia*, II. 575−6, WRO, Reg. Wyvil, I, fos. 15v−16r, HWRO, Reg. Montacute, pp. 142−4 (and for bishop's execution of king's 'premunientes' writ see p. 195), Norwich, D. & C. Muniments, Reg. X, fos. 1v−2r (prior's proxy), and BL, Cotton Vesp. E xxi, fos. 100v−101r.

[13] *Dignity of a Peer*, IV. 454−6, *Concilia*, II. 581 and Norwich, D. & C. Muniments, Reg. X, fos. 6v−7r.

[14] *Dignity of a Peer*, IV. 460−3, *Concilia*, II. 582−3, Wake, *State of the Church*, app. pp. 59−61 and HWRO, Reg. Montacute, pp. 177−9 (and for note of bishop's execution of king's 'premunientes' writ see p. 210).

[15] *Dignity of a Peer*, IV. 479−82, 495−6 and *Concilia*, II. 623 (CUL, EDR, Reg. Montacute, fo. 38).

York was addressed to the archbishop of York. A few, however — undoubtedly for parliaments — were addressed to the archbishop of Canterbury in response to provincial writs: for example, the proxies of the chapter of St Davids and of the clergy of St Davids for the parliament of May 1322, and the proxy of the chapter of Norwich for the parliament of February 1324.[16] Also, a proxy in a Bath register, from the subprior and chapter of Bath for the parliament of 1311, was addressed to the archbishop of Canterbury in reply to his summons to be at the parliament on 2 December. Other proxies for this assembly of 2 December, from Canterbury and from Worcester, although they too were certainly in response to the archbishop's summons, were addressed to the king.[17] Another, from the subprior and chapter of Rochester for the parliament of May 1322, while it was addressed to the king, made specific reference to the writs sent from the king to the archbishop and from the archbishop to the bishop.[18] And the chapter of Worcester's proxy for the parliament of July 1321 was also addressed to the king and also referred to the archbishop's citation. The prior of Worcester, for the same parliament, had two proxies drawn up, one addressed to the king and the other to the archbishop.[19] In the confusing situation of being summoned by both king and archbishop it appears not to have mattered at all whether the proxies were addressed to the one or to the other.

Yet, whether the clergy met before the king or before the archbishop was of crucial significance. In general, we can feel confident that any official reference to the clergy meeting 'coram archiepiscopo' should be regarded as a reference to an ecclesiastical assembly rather than to parliament. Largely for this reason assemblies before the archbishop on the day before parliament (26 January 1316) or on the same day as parliament (11 March 1330, 19 September 1334 and 11 March 1336) are regarded as provincial councils, separate from parliament and therefore requiring separate

---

[16] PRO SC10/8/358, /8/367 and /9/432. The vast majority of the proxies are apparently in response to the king's writ with the 'premunientes' clause, a number actually referring to the 'premunitio' and the bishop's citation: for example, C219/5/17/25 (see Appendix 1(i)), from the chapter of Worcester for the parliament of 19 Sept. 1334, like many from the Worcester diocese, reads 'iuxta formam vim et effectum premunitionis facte nobis in hac parte per venerabilem patrem dominum Simonem dei gratia Wygorniensem episcopum'.

[17] See below p. 108.

[18] PRO SC10/8/380.

[19] See below p. 112. n. 39.

proxies.[20] In the proxies mentioned above from the chapter and clergy of St Davids, for parliament but addressed to the archbishop, the term 'coram rege' or 'coram archiepiscopo' was avoided — as in many other proxies — and the proctors were appointed simply to be present in the king's parliament along with the archbishop, prelates, clergy and magnates. But an openly addressed proxy from the prior and chapter of Canterbury for the parliament of September 1314 appointed their cellarer to act for them 'coram archiepiscopo', and, likewise, an openly addressed proxy of the chapter of Norwich for the parliament of Salisbury in October 1328, which was in response, as it states, to the archbishop's mandate, appointed representatives to appear in the parliament 'coram archiepiscopo' and to treat there with the archbishop and clergy.[21] And there are other signs that those who formulated the letters of proxy at times believed that the clergy in parliament would treat specifically with the prelates and clergy there rather than with all those summoned to parliament. It is true that the proxies most often refer to the clerical proctors treating with, or consenting to those things to be ordained by, the common counsel either of the king or of the kingdom or of the prelates and magnates of the kingdom. But some stated that the representatives were to consent to those things ordained by the common counsel of the clergy or of the prelates and clergy,[22] or that they were to treat with the other clergy there present.[23] Also, the proxies frequently made reference to meeting with the clergy of their own province rather than with the clergy of the realm.[24] For instance, proctors of the York clergy for the parliament of January 1315 were appointed to treat with the archbishop of York in this parliament.[25] And a proxy from the clergy of the archdeaconry of Salop, which can only be for the parliament of 27 April 1309, called the forthcoming assembly a convocation of Robert Winchelsey, archbishop of Canterbury, and

[20] See below pp. 110 n. 32, 119 n. 56, 120 n. 58.
[21] *Parl. Writs*, II. ii. 128 and SC10/12/586 (and see /12/594).
[22] SC10/6/264 (parliament of May 1319), /8/357 (May 1322) and /9/450 (Feb. 1324).
[23] SC10/18/858, /870 (parliament of Feb. 1334), /19/944, see Appendix 1(k) (May 1335) and /18/879 (March 1336).
[24] All referring to the prelates or the clergy of the Canterbury province: SC10/2/51 (parliament of April 1309), LI, Hale 185, fo. 114r (Dec. 1311), *Parl. Writs*, II. ii. 139 and SC10/4/162 (Jan. 1315), /7/335 and *Parl. Writs*, II. ii. 237 (July 1321), SC10/8/358 and /367 (May 1322), /12/599 (Feb. 1329) and /21/1036 (March 1340).
[25] SC10/4/161.

his suffragan bishops, and the proctors were to consent to those things ordained 'coram ipsis'.[26] So, not only were the respective archbishops often required to summon their own clergy to parliament, but also there are clear indications that, within parliament itself, the clergy were in the habit, at least from time to time, of meeting in separate provincial assemblies.[27]

There seems no doubt that the actual procedure of election of representatives by the cathedral chapters and by the diocesan clergy was exactly the same whether the writs of summons came from the king or from the archbishop. In the case of the cathedral chapters the bishops, often through their officials, ordered the deans or priors and the chapters to respond to the terms of the summons. The Lichfield chapter objected strongly when the archdeacon of Stafford ordered the chapter to answer the summons to the ecclesiastical council of January 1329, pointing out that they could only be cited to appear by their dean;[28] but it was the archdeacon of Worcester (or his official) who was instructed by the bishop of Worcester (or his official) to summon the cathedral chapter.[29] This procedure in the diocese of Worcester may have been unusual. It seems that the deans or priors and the chapters were frequently summoned in one letter from the bishop addressed to both parties.[30] When the monks of Canterbury complained in 1332 that the archbishop had ordered the prior to summon the chapter, rather than summoning the chapter directly himself, the archbishop denied that there was any change in practice and claimed that the one method was in any case as good as the other.[31] Following the citations, meetings of the chapters were the occasion for the choosing of proctors, usually from among their own number. The Lichfield Chapter Act Book shows the process at work.[32] Canons were selected to be sent out on the business of this collegiate church, as to parliament or to ecclesiastical councils or to the Roman court. The number of days during which they were

---

[26] PRO C270/35/17 (see Appendix 1(c)).
[27] And see Denton, 'Clergy and parliament', pp. 94–5 and Denton, 'Reynolds and ecclesiastical politics', pp. 263–4.
[28] Bodl., Ashmole 794, fo. 24, and see *Reg. Martival*, e.g. II. i. 346–7, II. ii. 374. See also McHardy, 'Representation of clergy', p. 100.
[29] Worcester D. & C. Muniments, Liber Albus, fo. 51r.
[30] As *Reg. Baldock*, p. 42, *Reg. Woodlock*, p. 155, *Reg. Hethe*, p. 285 and *Reg. Greenfield*, I. 139, 146.
[31] *Lit. Cant.*, I. 438–43.
[32] Bodl., Ashmole 794, e.g. fos. 4v, 7r, 18v, 26r.

allowed to be non-resident had to be agreed. It was a practical matter of the interests of the church being defended in the world outside.

A majority of the proxies from the chapters of the cathedral churches were drawn up in the name of the chapter alone. This was always the case in the large number of examples which survive for Worcester and St Asaph, and in the smaller number for Lincoln and St Davids. The explanation is certainly not that the deans and priors always attended in person. In the case of Worcester the explanation may be that the chapter was summoned separately by the archdeacon. For some cathedral churches, notably Bath, Rochester and Coventry, the proxies were from the subprior and chapter. These must also be exclusively corporate proxies; the subprior was not being individually represented. But it appears that the representation of cathedral chapters in parliament does not present us with a clear and unmistakable illustration of corporate representation. The chapters very often named the same proctors as their deans or priors, and, not only this, they frequently did so in the one letter of proxy. This was always the case for the dean and chapter of Bangor, usually the case for the prior and chapter of Canterbury and for the prior and chapter of Ely, and often so for the dean and chapter of York. This did not necessarily mean that the one proxy served for both the prior or dean personally and at the same time for the chapter as a body, for even on occasions when both parties issued the one proxy there are examples of priors issuing, in addition, their own separate proxy, naming the same proctor or proctors.[33] Although chapters mostly issued their own separate letters of proxy and were acting to some extent independently of their heads, even so the distinction between the summons of the head of the chapter personally and of the chapter by one proctor does not seem to have been of great practical or constitutional significance. Chapters did not constitute perfect communities without their priors or deans.[34] Another indication of this is the statement in some of the proxies that the chapter's nomination had been made 'de consensu prioris' or 'de voluntate et consensu prioris' (Carlisle), or 'cum consensu et auctoritate prioris'

---

[33] Proxies for the prior and chapter of Bath and for the prior (March 1300: LI, Hale 185, fo. 81r), and for the prior and chapter of Ely and for the prior (March 1332: PRO SC10/15/742 and /743; May 1335: SC10/19/914 and /915).

[34] For heads of religious houses as representatives of their communities see Michaud-Quantin, *Universitas*, pp. 311–13.

(Worcester), or 'de licentia, consensu et mandato prioris' (Coventry).[35]

The election procedures for the clergy of the dioceses are certainly of much greater constitutional interest. Here corporate representation is not in any kind of doubt. There is one example of an individual along with the clergy of a diocese appointing the same proctors in the same letter of proxy: the archdeacon of Carlisle and the clergy of the city and diocese of Carlisle in 1315.[36] This was most unusual. The elections in the diocese of representatives of the clergy were probably not regarded as in any way remarkable, but it was, nonetheless, quite rare for the diocesan clergy to elect proctors for any other purpose than to attend ecclesiastical councils and parliaments.[37] Elections, as we shall see, were carried out in assemblies, sometimes large and sometimes — perhaps always in the Lincoln diocese — in each rural deanery. These were assemblies of those secular clergy who served the parishes, especially, of course, the rectors and vicars. Some proxies use general phrases to describe the constituency ('communitas totius cleri' and 'clerus et beneficiati');[38] the terms in some others are more specific but nevertheless all-embracing ('rectores et vicarii ac cetere persone ecclesiastice . . . que sub nomine cleri continentur' and 'rectores, vicarii, portionarii ceterique de clero').[39] The diocesan assembly ordered for an election by the bishop of Winchester in 1295 included abbots and priors as well as rectors and vicars.[40] And regular clergy were also summoned to take part in the election in the archdeaconry of Worcester in 1311: the official of the archdeacon was ordered, in the first place, to cite the individual abbots and priors, and, in the second place, to cite the rest of the religious of his archdeaconry with the clergy of the archdeaconry in order to elect a proctor for parliament.[41] But this inclusion of the regular clergy in the election

---

[35] SC10/9/435, /11/513, /18/856, /18/859, /18/894 and /19/910.

[36] SC10/4/157 (see Appendix 1(e)); and concerning the links between archdeacons and the parish clergy see below pp. 34, 46.

[37] See the proxy, dated 30 Sept. 1300, of the clergy of the city and diocese of Carlisle naming Henry de Sancto Nicholao as their proctor at Rome to negotiate revision of the assessment of ecclesiastical income for taxation purposes: *Reg. Halton*, I. 130–1. Another proxy, dated 14 Nov. 1301, of the bishop and the clergy of the city and diocese appointed M. Robert de Blencou to act for them in all cases and business concerning the bishop and churches of the diocese: *ibid.*, 169.

[38] SC10/2/61 and /1/38.

[39] SC10/11/509 and /1/28 (see Appendix 1(b)).

[40] *Reg. Pontissara*, p. 518.

[41] Worcester D. & C. Muniments, Liber Albus, fo. 51r (*Liber Albus*, p. 35).

process was apparently exceptional, despite the fact that monasteries possessed many appropriated churches and as *de iure* 'rectors' contributed to the expenses of the diocesan clergy's elected representatives.

Two main kinds of evidence shed light upon the process of election in the dioceses: the instructions by bishops to the archdeacons (or their officials) and the proxies. The orders to archdeacons were copied frequently into bishops' registers, and it is unnecessary to cite all the instances; but it should be noted at the outset that the evidence of the systematic summoning of the clergy in response to royal writs in some dioceses is a firm indication that the proxies which have survived are a small fraction of those issued. Let us take the diocese of Salisbury during the episcopate of Roger Martival (1315–30) as an example. No letter of proxy for the Salisbury clergy for the period 1295–1340 is apparently extant, though we know that one existed for the Carlisle parliament of 1307.[42] But Martival's register records the receipt and execution of mandates for a large majority of the parliaments and ecclesiastical councils held throughout his episcopate. Of the twenty-seven assemblies to which the lower clergy were summoned between 1316 and March 1330 the register contains mandates for all but six, and in most cases there is, at least, a note that the mandates were executed.[43] In seven cases, out of a possible eight, the archbishop's provincial writ of summons to parliament is also recorded. On twelve occasions the actual text of the bishop's letters to his archdeacons concerning the election of diocesan proctors was also copied into the register.[44] These letters were all in response to an ecclesiastical mandate, nine for an ecclesiastical council and three for a parliament. This fact simply reflects the method of compiling the register, or rather registers: the royal writs, with the 'premunientes' clause, were included in a separate register, and it was not thought necessary to include there anything more than a note of execution. In the diocese of Salisbury there were four archdeaconries, so that the bishop's letter was sent to each of four archdeacons. The instructions varied little from occasion to occasion. Each archdeacon was to summon the clergy of his archdeaconry who would elect a

---

[42] Below p. 105.

[43] See *Reg. Martival*, II and III passim.

[44] *Reg. Martival*, II. i. 49–50, 80, 146, 346, II. ii. 373–4, 389–90, 396–7, 423–4, 435–6, 529–30, 543, 596–7. A similar procedure had been followed by Martival's predecessor, Simon of Ghent: *Councils and Synods II*, pp. 1247, 1301, 1362.

proctor for the archdeaconry. The proctor should be given the power of appointing a substitute and should meet with the other three proctors in the cathedral church at Salisbury on a specified day in order to choose the proctors to represent the whole diocese.

There is no information for the diocese of Salisbury about how the archdeacons or their officials acted. Perhaps it is dangerous to assume that meetings of the clergy of whole archdeaconries took place, rather than separate meetings in each rural deanery. At any rate, the first elections had to be organised by the archdeacon or his official. The meeting at Salisbury of the four elected men may have opened up the possibility of episcopal influence over the final decision. The time allowed between the date of the bishop's letter and the meeting at Salisbury varied from six days to thirty-two days. On two occasions the archbishop's writ for a parliament arrived too late to be executed.[45] On one of these occasions, and probably on the other too, the king's writ had been received in good time and the lower clergy had probably already been summoned. It is curious that at no time do the bishop's letters concerning the archbishop's writs for parliaments refer to the king's 'premunientes' writ, which in some cases the register notes as having already been executed.[46] Either the bishop had in any case to go through all the formalities of executing the archbishop's mandate, or elections had to be ordered because the 'premunientes' clause had carried insufficient weight to ensure that proctors would be elected and sent. Sadly the evidence of the register is inconclusive on this crucial point. Nonetheless, all the indications are that writs were conscientiously executed. It is, however, worth noting that the bishop's certificate of execution of the archbishop's summons to the parliament of July 1321 was not sent because the summons was judged prejudicial, and it seems likely, too, that the clergy of Salisbury, like the bishop, were not represented at the parliament of May 1322 even though the bishop had ordered the execution of the archbishop's mandate.[47]

In the smallest of the dioceses the election procedure must have been relatively straightforward. For the six dioceses with only one archdeaconry few proxies survive, with the exception of Carlisle. None appears to have survived for this period from the diocese of Canterbury or from the diocese of Llandaff, only one from St

---

[45] *Reg. Martival*, II. ii. 541–2 (parliament of Sept. 1327), 579 (of Oct. 1328), and see III. nos. 720, 770.

[46] *Ibid.*, II. i. 346 (see III. no. 276), II. ii. 389–90 (see III. no. 329).

[47] *Ibid.*, II. i. 347, II. ii. 388–90, 394–8, *Parl. Writs*, II. ii. 259 and *Concilia*, II. 515–16.

Asaph, two from Ely and three from Rochester. These, and the ten from Carlisle, give little indication of the method of election, except that the use of the bishop's seal (or his official's or his vicar general's) for the proxies from Carlisle and Rochester could mean that the bishops there maintained control over the election process, whereas it was the seal of the archdeacon, on one occasion, and of the archdeacon's court on another, that was used in the diocese of Ely.[48] The episcopal registers which survive for Canterbury, Rochester and Carlisle are not very helpful, though ones for Rochester and Carlisle do show that the bishops in these dioceses ordered their own officials to execute the writs of summons.[49] For the Carlisle parliament of 1307 the diocese of Carlisle named four proctors, and three for the Northampton parliament of 1307; but thereafter the standard practice of electing two was adopted. It is possible that in all the dioceses with one archdeaconry a single assembly elected the representatives.[50] In dioceses with two arch-deaconries (Chichester, Durham, Hereford, Winchester and Worcester) the common procedure, it seems clear, was for the clergy of each archdeaconry to elect one proctor.[51] The proxies in

[48] Carlisle: *Reg. Halton*, I. 314 and PRO SC10/1/29, /4/157 (see Appendix 1(e)), /6/264, /8/357, /9/450, /15/701, /16/771, /18/862, /19/901; Rochester: SC10/3/149, /4/181, /11/509; Ely: SC10/1/33, /6/257. For the parliament of 1376 it was the bishop of Ely's official who held an assembly of the clergy of the diocese for the election of proctors: some of the clergy appeared in person, some by proctors and others were declared contumacious. For this election see Aston, *Arundel*, p. 409.

[49] *Reg. Hethe*, pp. 285−6 (for parliament of Nov. 1325); *Reg. Halton*, II. 58−9 (for Aug. 1312), CRO, Reg. Ross, p. 266 (for Sept. 1331) and CRO, Reg. Kirkby, pp. 348 (for March 1337) and 400 (for Jan. 1340).

[50] Bishop Halton's order to his offical in 1312 was for the convoking of the clergy of the whole diocese: *Reg. Halton*, II. 59.

[51] See the proxies in Appendix 5. Diocesan assemblies had been ordered by the bishop of Winchester for electing proctors in 1294 and 1295 (*Reg. Pontissara*, pp. 497, 518); but *Reg. Woodlock*, pp. 155−6, 206−7 (relating to the parliaments of 1307) confirms that the responsibility had come to rest with the clergy of each archdeaconry (Winchester and Surrey). For Jan. 1307 each archdeaconry elected two proctors; later evidence (for 1309, 1318 and 1321) shows each archdeaconry electing only one. In the Worcester diocese the evidence for Jan. 1307, 1319, Oct. 1328 and Nov. 1330 indicates separate archidiaconal responsibility for elections; but the proxy for Sept. 1334 came from the clergy of the whole diocese, and the keeper of the spiritualities ordered a diocesan assembly for the election of the two proctors for the parliament of Feb. 1339 (Worcester D. & C. Muniments, Sede Vacante Register, fo. 152r, calendared in *Reg. Sede Vacante*, p. 266).

these dioceses, with a few exceptions, were sent directly from the clergy of the archdeaconries. Also, the list of proctors at the Carlisle parliament indicates that something similar happened in the diocese of Norwich: the two archdeaconries of Suffolk and Sudbury combined to elect one proctor and the archdeaconries of Norwich and Norfolk combined to elect the other. The linking of the archdeaconries in this way is confirmed by the bishop of Norwich's mandates for the parliaments of 1311 and 1321 and for the ecclesiastical council of March 1336.[52]

In the largest dioceses matters were necessarily more complicated. The dioceses of Coventry and Lichfield and of York had five archdeaconries. The only proxies from the diocese of Coventry and Lichfield are for the 1309 parliament: one from the archdeaconry of Stafford and another from the archdeaconry of Salop, each naming the same two proctors. Nothing instructive has been found in the unprinted registers of Walter Langton and Roger Northburgh; but it is unlikely that proctors continued to be sent from each archdeaconry. The fourteen surviving proxies from York are all in the name of the clergy of the whole diocese and were authenticated with the seal of the official of the court of York; and the evidence relating to ecclesiastical councils indicates that the procedure was most probably for the election of proctors in each archdeaconry who then met before the archbishop for the election of two of them to represent the whole diocese.[53] This, as we have seen, was the pattern of events in the diocese of Salisbury, with its four archdeaconries. It was also certainly the pattern in the diocese of Lincoln, with its eight archdeaconries.[54] For Lincoln we have unusually detailed evidence. Letters from the officials of the archdeacons of Bedford and Northampton show that for the parliament of March 1300 each archdeaconry elected a proctor, and from the eight proctors two were chosen at a meeting (only, it seems, of the proctors themselves) which in this instance was held at Northampton before the official of Lincoln *sede vacante*.[55] Only two proxies are known from the clergy of the diocese of Lincoln. The first, for the parliament of 1305, was copied into Bishop Dalderby's register two folios after the copy of the bishop's execution of the royal writ.[56] The proctors from each archdeaconry had been ordered to

---

[52] Norwich D. & C. Muniments, Reg. IX, fos. 13v, 30v and Reg. X, fo. 7r.
[53] See *Councils and Synods II*, pp. 869, 981, 1094, 1128.
[54] See McHardy, 'Representation of clergy', pp. 104—5.
[55] Below p. 103 n. 11.
[56] LAO, Reg. III (Dalderby), fos. 77r, 79r.

meet with the bishop or his *locum tenens* on 16 January in the prebendal church of Grantham. This left, unusually, plenty of time — more than a month — before the date for which the parliament had been summoned. The proxy, with the bishop's seal, was dated 1 February at Liddington, some twenty-five miles south of Grantham. The second surviving proxy (for Carlisle 1307) is also in Dalderby's register, but the corresponding episcopal mandate for the election was not transcribed. We have only two proxies; but the copies, in the register, of Dalderby's mandates for every parliament (except Carlisle 1307) to which the lower clergy were summoned during his episcopate (1300−20) demonstrate his consistent and conscientious policy of ordering elections.[57] It should be stressed that these were episcopal *mandates* in response to the king's 'premunientes' writ. The supplementary archiepiscopal writs scarcely seem to have been necessary in the diocese of Lincoln. The execution of the provincial order for the parliament of 1315, for example, amounted to a confirmation of action already taken by the bishop.[58] About a month was allowed between the bishop's mandate and the meeting of the proctors from each archdeaconry; and there were a few favoured churches for this final meeting: Grantham, Stamford, Northampton, Huntingdon and Wigford.[59]

Additional evidence concerning the diocese of Lincoln from a Peterborough register, already noted by Maude Clarke, is of particular importance.[60] Here are archiepiscopal, episcopal and archidiaconal writs for the ecclesiastical councils held at Lincoln in January 1323 and at St Paul's in September 1334. The archidiaconal writs — in fact, of the official of the archdeacon of Northampton to all the rural deans of the archdeaconry — are rare survivals.[61] On

---

[57] *Ibid.*, fos. 77r, 121, 151r, 221r, 234, 255, 258r, 269, 275r, 281r, 302v, 309r, 334r, 395r, 413r−414r (and also fo. 292r for the parliament summoned to meet on 21 April 1314 but cancelled, and fos. 379v, 383v for parliaments in 1318 summoned but postponed).

[58] *Ibid.*, fo. 310v.

[59] The procedure was the same for ecclesiastical councils: *Councils and Synods II*, pp. 1248, 1293, 1362 n. 1.

[60] BL, Cotton Vesp. E xxi, fos. 50v−51v (*Parl. Writs*, II. ii. 281−2), and 100v−101r. See Clarke, *Representation*, p. 328.

[61] A mandate of the official of Surrey to the rural dean of Ewell may well have been concerned with the election of proctors for the ecclesiastical council of March 1297: see *Councils and Synods II*, pp. 1161−2. The Burton annalist's copy of a letter of 1257 from the official of Stafford to the rural dean of Tamworth and Tutbury unfortunately contains only the terms of the archiepiscopal and episcopal orders: *Councils and Synods II*, p. 531, cf. Clarke, *Representation*, p. 327.

these two occasions, and perhaps on most if not all others in the diocese of Lincoln, the responsibility for primary elections fell on the shoulders of the rural deans (ten in the archdeaconry of Northampton). The clergy of each rural deanery were required to send one proctor to a meeting before the official of the archdeacon, so that one could be selected to be sent to the episcopal meeting, so that two could be selected for the provincial council. How, then, was the election of the first proctor carried out in the rural deanery? The most likely answer is that the election took place in a meeting of the ruri-decanal chapter, either at one of its regular sessions, every three or four weeks, or at a specially convened session.[62]

Thus, no coherent pattern of electoral procedure throughout the realm is discernible. The whole process was on occasion, perhaps commonly in smaller dioceses, concluded in a diocesan assembly.[63] Or — maybe more usually than the evidence allows us to know — the primary and essential elections took place in the rural deaneries. Often, it is clear, the electoral constituency was the archdeaconry.[64] The episcopal mandates for the execution of writs of summons were for the most part addressed to the archdeacons or their officials. Rural chapters were under the control of archdeacons, who often presided there; and the chapters 'bore the same relationship to the archdeaconry as the county court did to the county'.[65] The counterpart of elections of knights of the shire in the county court was the election of clerical proctors in chapters of the archdeaconry.

From time to time bishops may well have had good reason — as well as the opportunity — to interfere in their clergy's choice of proctors; and prelates, cathedral clergy and diocesan clergy certainly sometimes worked together and named the same proctors.[66]

---

[62] For the frequency of the meetings of rural chapters see W. Dansey, *Horae Decanicae Rurales* (London, 1835), II. 5−6, 21−2, *Councils and Synods II*, pp. 615, 719, 1028, F. S. Pearson, 'Records of a ruridecanal court of 1300' in *Collectanea*, ed. S. G. Hamilton (Worcestershire Hist. Soc., 1912), pp. 68−81, *Provinciale*, ed. W. Lyndwood (Oxford, 1679), p. 14 (Lib. I, Tit. ii) and Clarke, *Representation*, p. 306. And see R. M. Haines, *The Administration of the Diocese of Worcester in the First Half of the Fourteenth Century* (London, 1965), pp. 67−8.

[63] Above p. 31 n. 51, and *Reg. Grandisson*, pp. 301−2 (election for the ecclesiastical council of Sept. 1337).

[64] See also Roskell, 'Consideration of *Modus*', pp. 421−2.

[65] J. Scammell, 'The rural chapter in England from the eleventh to the fourteenth century', *EHR*, 86 (1971), 20.

[66] Denton, 'Clergy and parliament', pp. 105−6.

When the bishop of Rochester's seal was appended to the proxy of
his diocesan clergy, dated at Bromley on 19 January 1315, he gave
his authority to the appointment of the same two proctors whom
he had named to act for him in his own proxy dated at Bromley on
18 January.[67] Yet there is little room to suspect that the parish
clergy were not in general free to appoint their own representatives.
Naming the same men was almost certainly more a matter of con-
venience than of interference. The bishop's seal was used to authen-
ticate some proxies; but this was, of course, subsequent to the election process.[68] It may be significant that we have found only three
proxies of diocesan clergy that were copied into episcopal
registers.[69] Above all, it is striking that the proctors were very frequently themselves beneficed clergy of their dioceses, and that they
acted in a single proctorial capacity more commonly than the proctors of bishops, archdeacons or cathedral clergy. Only two of the
fourteen proctors named by eight bishops to act for them at the
Carlisle parliament of 1307 were also named by the diocesan
clergy; and one of these proctors (Richard Woodloc, for the archdeaconry of Winchester) was among four named by the bishop and
three named by the clergy.[70] Generally speaking it is clear that the
diocesan clergy appointed their own men from among their own
number.

The elected men travelled to parliament with their sealed proxies.
The *Modus* stated[71] that they appeared at parliament with their
proxies in duplicate and that one was enrolled by the clerks of

67 PRO SC10/3/149, /4/153.
68 See the following note and SC10/3/149, /4/181 (sealed by the bishop of
Rochester), /4/157 (see Appendix 1(e)), /8/357, /19/901 (by the bishop
of Carlisle), and /11/511 (by the bishop of Durham). The diocesan
clergy had no common seal and their individual seals were not well
known (/2/61: 'quia sigilla nostra pluribus sunt incognita'). The *Modus*
noted that the duplicate warrants of the clerical proctors were sealed by
their superiors ('sigillis superiorum suorum signatis': *Parliamentary
Texts*, ed. Pronay and Taylor, p. 68), a common procedure by this time
(see Cheney, *Notaries*, p. 8). On occasion an archdeacon or cathedral
dean sealed a proxy, but more commonly it was the bishop's official or
the archdeacon's official. (For mention of the seal, rolls, registers and
muniments of the bishop's official see *Reg. Grandisson*, I. 12; and the
seal of the official of the archdeacon of Stow is described in *Reg.
Geynesborough*, p. 127.)
69 *Reg. Halton*, I. 314 and LAO, Reg. III (Dalderby), fos. 79 (printed in
Wake, *State of the Church*, app. p. 31) and 108v−109r.
70 *Parl. Writs*, I. ii. 184−6.
71 Above p. 13.

parliament[72] and the other was retained by the proctors. This may well have been the accepted procedure. The proxies are either openly addressed or addressed to the king (or, much more rarely, the archbishop), and A. K. McHardy has given examples, from later in the fourteenth century, of two surviving for the same appointment, one addressed openly and the other to the king.[73] It is tempting to assume that usually the former was retained by the proctor or proctors and the latter was presented to the clerks of parliament. But this can hardly have been the normal practice, for about two thirds of the proxies of the lower clergy in the Public Record Office — which must have been ones which were presented — are in fact openly addressed. So, if, as seems likely, proctors commonly appeared with duplicate warrants, they probably often had two identical proxies of the 'Universis pateat' or 'Noverint universi' sort.

But the form of the address mattered little. Exactly what powers were being granted mattered a great deal. It is well known that letters of proxy, for all kinds of work, administrative and judicial, general and particular, in the name of churchmen of every rank, abound in the bishops' registers and elsewhere. Very many related to legal actions or to negotiations in one court or another.[74]

---

[72] For a surviving enrolment of ecclesiastical proxies for the Carlisle parliament of 1307 see below p. 104 n. 15; and for two other enrolments see below p. 48 and n. 33. The archbishop's responsibility for examining proxies at the session of parliament convened for 2 Dec. 1311 is explained in his delegation of the duty in *Reg. Gandavo*, p. 417. But it was probably not always his responsibility at parliaments, for it was surely related on this occasion to the fact that the southern clergy had been summoned by the archbishop's provincial mandates, and, for this session of the 1311 parliament, by no other mandates. A letter from the prior of Durham refers to Michael de Wath (keeper of the rolls of Chancery, 1334 to 1337) as receiving the proxies in parliament: see Appendix 4.

[73] McHardy, 'Representation of the clergy', p. 101 n. 17. We have found no examples from the lower clergy for the period 1295–1340. There are three cases of enregistered copies of proxies surviving as well as the originals, from the chapter of Worcester in 1321 and 1322, and from the prior and chapter of Ely in 1335 (see Appendix 5); in all three cases the proxies are identical. But the bishop of Lincoln was in the habit of issuing two proxies, one openly addressed and the other addressed to the king: see below p. 68.

[74] For a formulary of proxies, with particular reference to representation in the Roman curia, see John of Bologna's *Summa Artis Notarie*. For the proxies given to his proctor at Rome by the bishop of Lincoln see *Reg.*

Representation in assemblies — ecclesiastical councils or parliaments — required a distinct and particular kind of proctorial letter. When the archbishop of York appointed William of Pickering to act for him at the parliament of Carlisle in the case to be heard there concerning the royal free chapel of Blyth *alias* Tickhill,[75] he gave to his agent proctorial powers which were quite different from those given to the other proctors appointed in response to the summons to parliament. Similarly, the bishop of Lincoln issued his proctors for the parliament of August 1311 with an additional proxy specifically to enable them to act for him in the presentation of articles of grievance from the bishops of the province.[76] Different circumstances of course meant that the form of proxies for assemblies did vary in some ways. A rector might appoint a proctor to fulfil various duties all specified in one proxy, such as taking oaths, and attendance at visitations and at diocesan assemblies;[77] or a bishop might appoint proctors for a succession of parliaments and councils, as did Bishop Pontoise of Winchester for the period of his absence from England.[78] Even so, there is no doubt that the warrants for the proctors in parliament were in a specific class.

Given all that has been written about the powers of representatives in parliament, students of the early history of parliament could be forgiven for believing in the central significance of the grant of 'full power'. The clauses of limitation in the proxies, declaring the purpose for which the representatives had been appointed, did often state that the proctors had been given 'full power' or 'full and free power' or 'full and sufficient power' or

---

Sutton, III. 78−81, VI. 13. Cuttino has analysed the procuratorial letters of English envoys on diplomatic missions in *Diplomatic Administration*, pp. 154−6, and see P. Chaplais, 'English diplomatic documents to the end of Edward III's reign' in *The Study of Medieval Records: Essays in Honour of Kathleen Major*, ed. D. A. Bullough and R. L. Storey (Oxford, 1971), esp. pp. 25−9, 40−3.

75 *Parl. Writs*, I. ii. 186; and see *Reg. Romeyn*, I. 331 and *Reg. Corbridge*, II. 59.

76 LAO, Reg. III (Dalderby), fo. 226v.

77 *Reg. Cobham*, p. 48.

78 *Reg. Pontissara*, pp. 330−1 (and see p. 781). And in October 1380 the prior of Worcester appointed proctors 'in quibuscunque consiliis congregationibus et parliamentis' assigned or to be assigned by the king, and 'in quibuscunque convocationibus consiliis et congregationibus', ordained or to be ordained by the archbishop: Wake, *State of the Church*, app. p. 76 (from Worcester D. & C. Muniments, Liber Albus, fo. 306v).

'special power'.[79] But such phrases were not, in fact, essential to the warrants. Certainly, a statement that the constituency or principal would accept whatever was done in their name was of prime importance, and this appears, in the vast majority of proxies,[80] in the *ratihabitio* or clause of guarantee ('ratum et gratum habituri quicquid . . .'). This is the grant of the power to act. It is important in any proxy and is not in the least exceptional. It can be quite properly called a grant of full power. But it must be stressed that this fullness of power was not a general grant allowing the proctors unlimited scope to act as they saw fit. The clause of guarantee appeared alongside the clause of limitation. The clause of limitation was the heart of the matter.[81] The proxies show that the clergy and the burgesses[82] — and also those who had been summoned individually but were absent[83] — sent their proctors specifically to treat, to act, to ordain and to give their consent (these terms were used in varying combinations)[84] concerning those matters which would be determined by common counsel. There is reflected here what E. A. R. Brown, following Gaines Post, has described as the balance between the ruler's desire for compliance and his subjects' determination to protect themselves. It must be said that it is not

[79] For special mandates see Post, *'Plena potestas* and consent', pp. 93—102.

[80] The clause is missing in a few proxies from Rochester, Carlisle and York (SC10/3/146, /18/867, /18/875—6, /19/934) and in a whole series from St Asaph (/4/162, /10/491, /12/577, /12/599, /15/721, /16/754, /19/903). This was probably an oversight. But there were certainly occasions when the omission of important clauses was without doubt deliberate: below pp. 68—9.

[81] For this clause in proxies see Brown, 'Representation and agency law', esp. pp. 333—9 and *eadem, 'Aide pur fille marier'*, pp. 11—18. There are few cases of proxies of the lower clergy without clauses of limitation, and these few cover themselves by specific reference to the terms of the writ of summons (as SC10/8/371 and /8/380) or even by citing the writ in full (/2/61).

[82] For the proxies of burgesses see above p. 14 n. 57.

[83] Detailed study of the many proxies of absent bishops, abbots and priors would possibly reveal some significant variations in the form of the letters; but those in print for the parliament of Feb. 1324 (*Parl. Writs*, II. ii. 293—9) suggest that absent prelates gave essentially the same powers to their proctors as did the lower clergy. For the unusual proxies of Bishop Dalderby of Lincoln, see below p. 68. For the proxies of magnates see Roskell, 'Problem of attendance', p. 173.

[84] For discussion of the power to 'treat' see Post, *'Plena potestas* and consent', pp. 118n, 155—6.

easy to see how these proctorial powers were used in practice; and we shall return to an examination of the terms of the proxies both in relation to the attendance of the proctors and in relation to their political influence in parliament. But it can be stated without equivocation that the power of the elected representatives was rooted in the grant by their constituents, responding to the royal summons, that they would accept as binding what was to be agreed to in common counsel.

3

Attendance

Arguments for the extensive non-attendance of the knights and the burgesses have been largely disposed of.[1] On the other hand, opinion concerning the lower clergy in parliament, although admitting of some doubts,[2] remains on the side not only of the withdrawal of the clergy from parliament during the 1330s[3] but also of the irregularity of attendance of the lower clergy, with no established pattern of election and representation.[4] How far can we accept this belief in the poor attendance, and in the dwindling attendance, of the lower clergy? A. K. McHardy has already shown, for the period 1340 to 1400 that 'the lower clergy were more assiduous in undertaking their parliamentary duties than has been assumed hitherto'.[5]

The first matter to be cleared up concerns the number of representatives appointed in the letters of proxy. The king asked for cathedral chapters to elect one and diocesan clergy to elect two proctors; but frequently more than the required number were appointed. This practice puzzled Prynne long ago when he examined the returns to parliament of the city of London; he found that some proxies appointed three or four citizens when the writ of summons had called for only two.[6] Likewise, the clergy of Carlisle

---

[1] Edwards, 'Personnel of the Commons', pp. 197–214, McKisack, *Representation of Boroughs*, pp. 66–81 and Roskell, 'Problem of attendance', p. 153 n. 1 & App. A.

[2] Note the comment in the introduction to the list of parliaments in Powicke and Fryde (eds.), *Handbook of British Chronology*, p. 496: 'No attempt has been made after 1327 to indicate the presence or absence of the representatives of the diocesan clergy. This is a matter demanding further research.'

[3] See above p. 2 n. 4.

[4] As stated in *Parliamentary Texts*, ed. Pronay and Taylor, p. 42.

[5] McHardy, 'Representation of clergy', p. 107.

[6] *Brief Register*, ed. Prynne, III. 377. It is clear, however, that with the

appointed four proctors for the parliament of Carlisle in January 1307. After the early years of Edward II's reign the appointment of only two from each diocese became the generally established pattern. But the naming by some cathedral chapters of two, or more, proctors continued to be common practice. It seems unlikely that the king was greatly concerned about the actual numbers of representatives sent to parliament by each constituency during the period under review here. The requirement of one from each chapter (in addition to the dean or prior) and two from each diocese was probably understood by all concerned as an attempt to ensure, without imposing too great a burden, that each constituency was represented. The naming of more than one attorney in the king's courts was a common precaution,[7] and the reason for it was stated clearly in Ralph of Hengham's *Summa Magna* as security against illness, death or even deception: 'securum est . . . facere duos attornatos pro periculo infirmitatis seu mortis vel etiam fraudis'.[8]

The fact that many of the proxies named more than the required number of proctors shows that the constituencies, as well as the king, were concerned to ensure that representation did take place. This is also the implication of a statement in the proxy of the clergy of Carlisle for October 1307: three proctors were appointed and the clergy agreed to accept whatever was done by the said proctors 'coniunctim seu duo vel unus'. Similarly, the proxy for the Durham clergy for November 1325 appointed two proctors to act for them 'sub alternatione'.[9] In both cases one man could do the job, even though two men had been summoned. This must also have been intended by the use of the phrase 'coniunctim et divisim et utrum eorum insolidum' by the Rochester clergy for January 1315, January 1316 and November 1325,[10] and also, indeed, by the use of the simple phrase 'coniunctim et divisim' by the Bath and Wells clergy for October 1307, by the archdeacon and clergy of Carlisle for January 1315 and by the St Davids clergy for May 1322.[11]

---

exception of London, the general practice of naming two knights of the shire and two burgesses was already firmly established by the time of the Carlisle parliament of 1307: *Parl. Writs*, I. ii. 187—90.

[7] *Introduction to the Curia Regis Rolls 1199—1230*, ed. C. T. Flower (Selden Soc. 62, 1943), pp. 401—2.

[8] *Radulphi de Hengham Summae*, ed. W. H. Dunham (Cambridge, 1932), p. 18.

[9] PRO SC10/1/29 and /11/511.

[10] SC10/3/149, /4/181 and /11/509.

[11] SC10/1/20 (see Appendix 1(a)), /4/157 (see Appendix 1(e)), and /8/367.

Representation was important. Numbers were a safeguard. And they were perhaps a safeguard in several ways, for the practice of co-proctorship, which often operated alongside the practice whereby principals or constituencies named the same proctors, may well, as we shall see, have increased the possibility of each principal or constituency being separately represented. And it should be noted that to argue against the significance of numbers as such is at least to weaken any suggestion that one group was more important in parliament than another merely because it was larger.[12]

The appointment of a number of attorneys 'disjunctively', so that if necessary only one could act, was referred to in Britton, the legal treatise of c. 1291, and it had been specifically defined by Bracton: 'constituti enim sunt attornati sub disjunctione ita quod si unus non venerit vel venire non possit quod alius veniat'.[13] The same principle probably applied in parliament as in other royal courts. A large number of the proxies of chapters named only one man; but about two thirds of all those of the lower clergy which named more than one man contain some kind of 'disjunctive' clause. In these clauses certain phrases re-occur in varying combinations: 'coniunctim et divisim' and 'quemlibet eorum insolidum' and 'sub alternatione' and 'ita quod non sit melior conditio occupantis'. A distinction between 'insolidum' and 'sub alternatione' has been indicated in some proctorial appointments for legal representation, the former signifying that one or more might act without any other and the latter that two should act in turn.[14] But that the two phrases in parliamentary proxies were not always mutually exclusive is suggested by a proxy of the Lincoln chapter for the parliament of April 1309, which appointed two proctors 'sub alternatione, videlicet quemlibet eorum insolidum'.[15] If there were distinctions between the two phrases, the aim in linking them together was perhaps to ensure greater flexibility. Other clauses were also linked together: proxies of the York chapter for February 1339 and March 1340 appointed, respectively, two and four proctors 'coniunctim et

---

12 Concerning the changes implied by the Modus in the numbers of representatives of the lower clergy in parliament cf. Roskell, 'Consideration of Modus', pp. 419—22 and Denton, 'Clergy and parliament', p. 105 n. 57.

13 Britton, ed. F. M. Nichols (Oxford, 1865), II. 358 and Bracton, ed. Woodbine, IV. 86.

14 Sayers, Judges Delegate, p. 230.

15 PRO SC10/2/54.

quemlibet eorum divisim per se insolidum'.[16] Matters of procedure concerning proctors in legal cases were clarified by Boniface VIII in the *Sext*.[17] There we learn that if the word 'insolidum' was not used in the letter of appointment one proctor should not be admitted without the other. When appointed 'insolidum' the first to undertake the affair should be recognised, and the other could not take over unless it was stated in the letter of appointment 'quod non sit melior conditio occupantis'. This suggests that the use of this latter phrase in some of our letters of proxy was perhaps an additional safeguard or refinement, ensuring that if one proctor was unable to continue for whatever reason another could take his place. Thus, the Ely clergy appointed two proctors for October 1318 'coniunctim et divisim et utrum eorum insolidum ita quod non sit occupantis melior conditio', as also did the Rochester chapter for March 1313 and the Norwich chapter for October 1328.[18] The proxy for the prior and chapter of Ely for July 1321 used the same combination of phrases and continued: 'quod unus eorum inceperit alter libere poterit adimplere'.[19]

It seems unlikely that the use or non-use of these different 'disjunctive' clauses in the proxies for parliament was a critical matter. The clauses, rather than enabling us to distinguish with confidence between the rights of different sets of proctors, illumine what was in general the way in which the representatives proceeded. To put it simply, they could act either together or one at a time. Flexibility was important. A good number of the proxies also included clauses which allowed the proctors to appoint substitutes.[20] We know that substitutes were appointed by some of the proctors at the Carlisle parliament of 1307, and those who substituted were specifically described as possessing the power of substitution.[21] It is possible, though we cannot be certain, that this power had to be granted in the letter of proxy.[22]

---

[16] SC10/21/1032, /22/1086.

[17] *Sext*, 1. 19. 6 (discussed in Queller, *Office of Ambassador*, p. 56).

[18] SC10/6/257, /2/100 (see Appendix 1(d)) and /12/586.

[19] SC10/7/325 (see Appendix I(g)).

[20] SC10/2/100 (see Appendix I(d)), /4/176, /5/248, /6/256, /6/257, /6/290, /7/341 etc.

[21] *Parl. Writs*, I. ii. 186.

[22] There was a tradition in English law that an attorney could not make an attorney or an agent make an agent: *Bracton*, ed. Woodbine, IV. 145. While ecclesiastical proctors 'ad negotia' could, as declared in *Sext*, 1, 19, 1, freely appoint deputies, the proxies 'ad negotia et ad causas' in the *Summa Artis Notarie*, of John of Bologna, pp. 615—18, had included specific grants of the power of substitution.

Letters in a Canterbury register relating to the parliament of January 1327, which witnessed the deposition of Edward II, demonstrate the sort of problems hinted at by the terms of the proxies.[23] The proxy of Christ Church Canterbury for this parliament employed the phrase 'coniunctim et divisim'. On 3 January the prior wrote to the archbishop of Canterbury, excusing himself from attendance at the forthcoming parliament for reasons known to the archbishop and expressing confidence, on his own behalf and on behalf of the chapter of Canterbury, in what would be ordained by the counsel and consent of the archbishop and the bishops and clergy of the Canterbury province. He informed the archbishop that brother Geoffrey Poterel and Hugh de Byssopestone, the archbishop's own clerk, would appear as the chapter's proctors on the first day of the parliament. But the prior asked, on behalf of the monks of Canterbury, that Geoffrey Poterel, the priory's almoner, be allowed as quickly as possible to return home to protect his property because of the archbishop's wish to be accommodated in a residence belonging to the álmoner. The prior also wrote to Hugh de Byssopestone telling him that because it was feared that the parliament would last a long time he had been appointed proctor at the forthcoming parliament along with Geoffrey Poterel. For some parliaments the prior and chapter had on occasion named only one proctor.[24] The prior went on to inform Hugh that it was not convenient for Geoffrey to stay a long time in London and to request him to take the place of Geoffrey when he left. Practical and necessary arrangements of this kind lie behind the 'disjunctive' clauses in the proxies.

Another problem, related to the question of numbers, arises from the fact that many clerical proctors, at the same time as being very frequently co-proctors, were named to represent more than one principal. This is clear from the surviving proxies. For example, Walter de Lugwardyn was named to represent the bishop of Hereford, the archdeacon of Hereford and the chapter of Hereford at the Northampton parliament of October 1307, and, even more notably, David Fraunceys was named for the York parliament of 1322 as a proctor for the bishop of St Davids, each of the four archdeacons of the diocese, the cathedral chapter and the diocesan clergy.[25] The list of proctors for the Carlisle parliament of

[23] *Lit. Cant.*, I. 203–4 and *Parl. Writs*, II. ii. 354.
[24] As in 1318, 1321 and 1324: *Parl. Writs*, II. ii. 185, 237, 294.
[25] PRO SC10/1/19, /1/35 and /1/37. And see Denton, 'Clergy and parliament', pp. 105–6.

1307 provides a better indication of the extent of this practice than the extant proxies which are clearly relatively rare survivors. This Carlisle list of proctors was, it seems, regarded as complete, though it may be that some who arrived late were not included, for it is not known precisely when the list was compiled. It presents some immediate problems as a source for assessing attendance at the parliament. The proctors of individuals mark, of course, the absence of those individuals; yet, it would certainly be dangerous to assume that all the individuals for whom no proctors are noted were in attendance. The list was drawn up, there can be little doubt, from the proxies which were presented; but the presentation of proxies does not prove that all the proctors named were present.

Fifteen out of a possible twenty-three cathedral chapters[26] are listed as having sent proctors. Six of the fifteen named only one proctor, four of whom (for London, Ely, Chichester and York) were single capacity proctors, that is they were appointed by no other principal. Of the nine chapters which named more than one proctor, six named at least one single capacity proctor. Thus, out of the fifteen chapters, ten were represented by at least one single capacity proctor and five were represented only by multiple capacity proctors (Rochester, Exeter, Salisbury, Norwich and St Asaph). To look at the evidence another way, the fifteen chapters named a total of twenty-five proctors: twelve were single capacity proctors, five were named by one other principal (two of these were the cathedral prior in a separate proxy, two were the bishop of the diocese and one was the diocesan clergy), five were named by three other principals, two by four other principals and one by five other principals. The prelates and clergy of the very poor diocese of St Asaph had great difficulty sending a large number of proctors: the same two men were named by the chapter, the dean and the archdeacon together, and the clergy; and the bishop of St Asaph named one of the same and added a third. And the distant Exeter chapter named one man who was also named, alone, by the bishop of Exeter and by the archdeacon of Wells. This last case is a rare example of a proctor representing clergy outside the one

---

[26] Rochester mysteriously appears twice, appointing a different proctor. This is not a misreading of PRO C153/1 fo. 131r but could be a scribal error. The missing chapters are three of the Welsh chapters (Llandaff, Bangor, St Davids), Bath, Coventry, Lichfield, and surprisingly Carlisle, and also Canterbury, for the archbishop was suspended from office and no summons is recorded as having been sent to the papal keepers of the spiritualities, William Testa and William Géraud de Sore (see *Parl. Writs*, I. ii. 182 and Denton, *Winchelsey*, p. 240).

diocese. Although there are a few royal clerks among the chapters' proctors (William de Thorntoft, for Worcester, Adam de Osgodby, canon of York, for York, and Robert de Pykering, canon of Lincoln, for Lincoln, all of them single capacity proctors), it is clear that in most cases the proctors came from, or were closely associated with, the chapters' own dioceses. While a large number of the proctors were multiple capacity proctors, in most dioceses distinct and independent representation was possible.

At first glance the representation of the diocesan clergy appears very similar to that of the cathedral chapters. No proxies were sent, it seems, from the chapters of six dioceses, and the clergy of the same dioceses, excepting only Carlisle, did not send proxies, that is Llandaff, Bangor, St Davids, Coventry and Lichfield, and Canterbury. And again there are multiple capacity proctors. The chapters of five dioceses were represented only by multiple capacity proctors, and, substituting Ely for Exeter, the same was true for the clergy of these dioceses. Yet, the incidence of multiple capacity proctors is, in fact, lower for the diocesan clergy than for the chapters. Out of a total of thirty-seven, sixteen were multiple capacity proctors: forty-three per cent as compared with fifty-two per cent for the chapters. Separate representation was possible in eleven out of the sixteen dioceses: seven had named proctors who were all single capacity proctors and there was at least one single capacity proctor from each of a further four dioceses. Another factor is of interest: all but three of the sixteen multiple capacity proctors were named by absent archdeacons as well as by the diocesan clergy, and seven were named only by an archdeacon in addition to the diocesan clergy. Of all the ecclesiastical dignitaries it was the archdeacon (or his official, for many archdeacons were absentees) who had the closest links with the local clergy: we have seen that the rural chapter where the election of representatives of the clergy often took place was under the archdeacon's supervision, and archdeacons had been clearly responsible for representing the interests of the parish clergy before a system of elected representatives was established in the second half of the thirteenth century.[27]

The description by the chronicler Bartholomew Cotton of how the clergy, in the Bury St Edmunds parliament of 1296, divided into separate groups in order to discuss a proposed tax enables us to examine in a different way the evidence from the Carlisle parliament. Cotton tells us that the clergy divided into four groups: the

[27] Above p. 34 and Denton, 'Clergy and parliament', p. 96.

archbishop of Canterbury (the archbishop-elect of York had not received his temporalities and was not summoned) and the bishops and proctors of absent bishops; the abbots, priors and other monks; all the ecclesiastical dignitaries ('omnes in dignitatibus constituti'); and the proctors of the diocesan clergy ('procuratores communitatis cleri').[28] The monks can be separated from the others, for the proctors of the parliamentary abbots were almost always single capacity proctors and there is no doubt that the monks were in a 'gradus' distinct from the secular clergy;[29] but it should be noted that it was in this group that the priors and chapters of monastic cathedrals must have been represented. With bishops on their own and parish clergy on their own, it is plain that the deans and archdeacons and the chapters of the secular cathedrals met together in the one grouping. This may not always, of course, have been the way in which discussion was organised, though the same divisions were certainly used again in the ecclesiastical councils of January and March 1297.[30] Keeping in mind this rare piece of evidence from the reliable Cotton about how matters were arranged in parliament, we can ask whether there were enough proctors named by the clergy for the Carlisle parliament to ensure that each constituency would be represented in groupings of this kind. Clearly there would have been some difficulties, arising almost entirely from the fact that for the dioceses of Salisbury, Chichester, Worcester and Norwich the same proctors had been appointed to represent the parish clergy and also absent archdeacons. But this problem apart — and noting also that the same one man represented the bishop of Exeter and the chapter of Exeter — it is a surprising fact that the large number of multiple capacity proctors has not prevented a high degree of representation from taking place, always assuming that most of the named proctors had appeared. In effect, the practice of naming more than one proctor could have largely counteracted the problems caused by multiple capacity proctorship. And if it was not thought necessary for the dean, chapter and archdeacons of a diocese always to have a representative each in the one grouping, then the problems disappear almost entirely. The representation of the clergy in parliament was

[28] *Bartholomaei de Cotton Historia Anglicana*, ed. H. R. Luard (RS, 1859), pp. 314—15 and *Councils and Synods II*, p. 1150.

[29] *Ibid.*, pp. 1203—4 (letter from archbishop of Canterbury in 1301): 'cum . . . nec in gradu cleri possint religiosi, quoniam certum gradum per se habuerunt in omnibus convocationibus nostris ita quod non teneantur cum clero contribuere, aliqualiter computari . . .'.

[30] *Ibid.*, pp. 1158, 1161, 1166 and see Clarke, *Representation*, pp. 322—3.

certainly not straightforward, but this is not to say that it was ineffective.

Taking the chapters and diocesan clergy together, seventy-two per cent of the constituencies of the lesser clergy that were summoned (there is no record of the summons of the cathedral and clergy of Canterbury) sent proxies for the Carlisle parliament. If we exclude the Welsh dioceses from the reckoning, which puts the clergy almost on a par topographically with the summoned knights of the shire, then the percentage of constituencies which sent proxies rises to eighty-three per cent. A large shortfall is created by the fact that there were no proxies listed from Coventry and Lichfield with its five archdeaconries and its two cathedral chapters; excluding Coventry and Lichfield from the reckoning increases the percentage of those responding to the summonses to ninety-three per cent. These figures are to be compared with the number of sheriffs' returns, and the list drawn up from them, which indicate that only Northamptonshire made no return.[31] Neither the list of proxies received nor the list of sheriffs' returns is necessarily an accurate guide to the actual attendance of the named clerical or lay representatives. But we can surely be confident that the clerical proxies were carried to parliament by either the named proctor or one of the named proctors. The letters of the Winchester chapter in 1318, of the Lincoln chapter in 1325 and 1327, of the clergy of the archdeaconry of Worcester in 1328 and of the dean and chapter of Bangor in 1330 described their proctor as 'exhibitor presentium'.[32]

There are at least two other surviving lists of received proxies: a list of members for the parliament of October 1307, which appears to have been left incomplete, since spaces follow the list of proctors from the parish clergy and also the list of proctors appointed by three abbots; and a mutilated list for the parliament of February 1324, on which the only surviving ecclesiastical entries are the proctors of the bishop and of the chapter of St Asaph.[33] We cannot

---

[31] The list as printed in *Parl. Writs*, I. ii. 187–90 and *Return of Members*, I. 24–6, and also a partial list surviving as PRO C49/68/4, need to be compared in detail with the returns (E175/1/21) which provide additional information (see Sayles, 'Parliamentary representation in 1294, 1295 and 1307', p. 111). For the significance of the dots and crosses against names on the list see Roskell, 'Problem of attendance', p. 161 n. 1.

[32] SC10/6/256, /11/521, /12/572, /14/667, and see Appendix 2 and below p. 114 n. 44.

[33] PRO C49/4/1 (and it includes the names of bishops, apparently those present; and see below p. 106 n. 19), and *Parl. Writs*, II. ii. 311.

know whether the Carlisle list is typical or atypical. But it is plain that all the extant proxies and copies of proxies are but a fraction of those which were sent to parliament after parliament by the lesser clergy. Thirty-six proxies are listed for Carlisle. The most to have actually survived, as originals or copies, for other parliaments are as follows: seventeen for January 1315, fourteen for November 1325, thirteen for May 1322 and February 1324, twelve for October 1307 and ten each for October 1318, May 1319 and February 1334. Two factors strongly indicate that these are far from being complete totals. As Appendix 5 shows, the names of proctors (excluding the evidence for the Carlisle parliament) are derived from 181 extant proxies in the Public Record Office, supplemented by other evidence, mainly copies of proxies in cathedral registers. There are forty-nine items of additional evidence, but only four of these items duplicate the evidence from the original proxies. There are only three cases of the survival of both the enregistered copy of a proxy and the original. And it is noteworthy that while the registers of Christ Church Canterbury provide copies of proxies, or memoranda concerning proxies, for nineteen parliaments, not a single original proxy from Canterbury is extant. On the other hand, there are many originals, as for Worcester and Durham, for which there are no copies in the surviving registers. There was no systematic enregistering of proxies, and, if there was systematic filing of proxies brought to parliament, only a few of these are extant. The second indication that the sending of proxies was much more extensive and regular than the direct evidence might suggest is found in bishops' registers. We have already seen that in two dioceses for which there are carefully compiled registers (Salisbury and Lincoln) there is evidence of a very conscientious response to the royal and archiepiscopal writs.[34] Although we have very few proxies, or references to proxies, from the clergy of these dioceses (one from Salisbury and two, both in the bishop's register, from Lincoln), it is probable that there were few parliaments to which proctors were not sent. In short, the complement of clerical proctors may have been at least as great at most parliaments as it was at Carlisle.

Yet, with the exception of the parliaments for which there was, or probably was, an archiepiscopal mandatory summons (September 1314, January 1315, January 1316, July 1321, May 1322 and February 1324),[35] the summons to parliament of the lower clergy was not by enforceable writs. The clergy were not bound to attend.

[34] Above pp. 29—34.
[35] Above p. 21.

One reason, perhaps the main reason, for resorting to the additional archiepiscopal citations was to secure complete or near complete attendance. The king's mandates to the archbishops in the last years of Edward II's reign specifically refer to a desire to prevent the absence of the clergy, and for the period 1327 to 1340 the writs to the archbishops refer to the ineffectiveness of the 'premunientes' summons. So attendance, however high or low, cannot have been satisfactory to the Crown. The clergy often stated that the king could not compel them to go to parliament, a secular court. This was one of the matters stressed by the clergy in their detailed complaints in 1314—16 and in 1323; and it was stated again in 1341, 1356 and 1363.[36] There is no evidence to corroborate the statement in the *Modus* that if proctors of the clergy did not attend parliament the bishops were fined one hundred marks for each archdeaconry in default.[37] Punishment of the clergy for non-attendance could only be a possibility if they refused to obey archiepiscopal or episcopal mandates: archbishops, for example, might punish failure to respond to a summons to an ecclesiastical council ('archiepiscopus graviter puniet non parentes').[38]

Can we know how far a lack of legal duress actually affected the attendance of the clergy? The matter of attendance at parliament was discussed by the bishop of Worcester's council in 1300: 'concerning proctors to be sent to the king's parliament let the bishop, by reason of his barony, send there an essoiner and proctor, if it be necessary, and let the bishop's official cause the royal writ to be explained to the prior and chapter, the archdeacons and the clergy but let him not induce ('inducat') anyone to go to London'.[39] In 1311 proxies were drawn up for the prior and chapter of Worcester following the king's summons of the clergy to a parliament on 8 August, but no proxies were taken to parliament until there had been an archiepiscopal summons four months later. In the priory of Worcester's register appears this note: 'the proxies were not delivered because the clergy are not bound to obey a royal summons without a mandate of the archbishop'.[40] Thus in 1311, if not

---

[36] See Denton, 'Reynolds and ecclesiastical politics', pp. 257—74, *idem*, '*Communitas cleri*', pp. 72—8, Clarke, *Representation*, pp. 23, 25, 139, *Concilia*, II. 517, Chew, *Ecclesiastical Tenants-in-Chief*, p. 174 and McHardy, 'Representation of clergy', p. 105.

[37] *Parliamentary Texts*, ed. Pronay and Taylor, p. 71.

[38] *Reg. Martival*, II. ii. 373, 543.

[39] Clarke, *Representation*, pp. 129—30, from HWRO, Reg. Giffard, attachment to fo. 442 (inadequately calendared in *Reg. Giffard*, II. 515).

[40] Below p. 108 n. 25.

also in 1300, actual attendance from the Worcester diocese was reduced because the king could only 'forewarn' the clergy.

The use of archiepiscopal mandates for parliament did not, however, necessarily improve the attendance figures. When the king's summons was bolstered by the archbishop's mandate, as for January 1315 and July 1321, we have evidence that at least some of the bishops regarded the mandate as prejudicial and did not respond to it. The bishop of Exeter sent no certificate of execution in 1315 and the bishop of Salisbury likewise in 1321.[41] It is difficult to judge how serious was this disaffection: for in 1315 it was stated in the bishop of Exeter's register that the other bishops sent their certificates of execution, but the note in the bishop of Salisbury's register informs us that in 1321 there were other bishops who did not wish to certify to the execution of the mandate.

Another factor of importance emerges in 1322, when the clergy of the southern province were summoned (once again by the archbishop's mandate as well as the royal writ) to meet in the northern province. Because of the absence of the clergy of some dioceses it was necessary to summon an ecclesiastical council, and the archbishop of Canterbury's letter of summons to the council makes it clear that it was a large number of the representatives of the lower clergy of the southern province that had been absent from the parliament, even though ten of the seventeen bishops of the province had been present and the other bishops had been absent for good reason.[42] The archbishop admitted that the clergy could not be compelled by him to attend a place outside the province of Canterbury and stated that the warrants given to the proctors of the clergy who were present did not seem to be sufficient to do what was necessary.[43] This last assertion perhaps simply meant that it was judged improper that the proctors who were present should bind to a new tax the constituencies that had not sent proctors. The same problem arose in reverse when the clergy of the York province were summoned to Lincoln in the autumn of 1327; the

---

[41] *Reg. Stapeldon*, p. 122, *Reg. Gandavo*, pp. 550–1 and *Reg. Martival*, II. i. 347.

[42] Wake, *State of the Church*, app. p. 47, *Concilia*, II. 516, *Parl. Writs*, II. ii. 259, Clarke, *Representation*, p. 144 n. 3 and *Reg. Martival*, II. ii. 394–8.

[43] 'Verum quia magna pars cleri a loco tractatus tunc abfuit, ad quem venire tanquam extra suum territorium, provinciam videlicet Cantuariensem, compelli minime potuit de iure, mandataque procuratoribus cleri tunc presentibus facta ad actum de quo agebatur sufficere minime videbantur . . .'.

archbishop of York reported that few of the clergy of his diocese and province had been present and he accepted as legitimate the claim of those present that the clergy were not bound to appear outside their own province.[44] This same claim was stressed in a run of very unusual proxies from the clergy of the York diocese for four parliaments at Westminster between 1339 and 1341.[45] In these letters the proctors were appointed only for the purpose of excusing the attendance of the clergy. But these were more publicists than essoiners. If the York clergy had wished it, their essoiners could no doubt have acted as their proctors. These proxies were intended to demonstrate the importance that the lower clergy attached to the privilege of attending parliament only at their own discretion, especially when it was held outside their own province.

A letter from the prior of Durham, sent, it seems likely, to a proctor appointed by the prior and chapter of Durham for the parliament of May 1335, cannot be related to the same issue, for the parliament was to meet in York.[46] The prior wrote that two proxies had been drawn up and were to be used if necessary. Past experience had taught him that it was not necessary to show such proxies nor indeed to appear in parliament, but if his addressee had heard any recent information on the matter he should act accordingly. The prior was taking no risks, and his letter shows not only that it was impossible to compel attendance but also, and perhaps as a result, that proxies were probably not being systematically received. And yet, the proctor, using his discretion, did think it wise or proper to deliver the proxy.[47]

Whether there was a reduction during the 1330s in the number of the lower clergy attending parliament is not easy to assess. Maude Clarke overstated the case.[48] Whatever was claimed by the clergy in support of their rights, some southern clergy did continue to attend parliament in the northern province and *vice versa*; and the fact that the proctors of the lower clergy were last mentioned on the rolls of parliament in 1332 tells us very little about short-term

---

[44] *Historical Papers*, ed. Raine, pp. 344–5 (from York, Borthwick Institute, Reg. Melton, fo. 468r, calendared in *Reg. Melton*, I. 89) and Clarke, *Representation*, p. 145.

[45] PRO SC10/21/1025, /22/1064, /22/1098 (see Appendix 1(l)) and /23/1113, and see Kemp, *Counsel and Consent*, p. 105 n. 2.

[46] Appendix 4.

[47] SC10/19/929 (see Appendix 1(j)).

[48] T. F. T. Plucknett went even further and argued that the bishops and archbishops failed to respond to the king's writs to summon the lower clergy: 'Parliament', p. 100.

trends, and certainly should not persuade us to give special emphasis to the year 1332.[49] Even so, the clergy do seem to have become
more recalcitrant. When the question of further taxation was in the
air there are indications that the clergy were absent in large
numbers, and no doubt deliberately so. And during the 1330s it
became a regular procedure to have separate ecclesiastical
assemblies convoked to work in co-operation with parliaments.[50]
Attempts to tax the clergy in parliament were being abandoned. All
this did not amount to anything approaching complete secession
from parliament, and there was probably no intention on the part
of the Crown or the clergy that there should be total withdrawal.
Certainly by 1340 convocations of clergy had become quite
separate from parliament, and taxes were granted there; but the
lower clergy continued to be summoned to both. There is no
evidence up to 1340 that absenteeism, however great or small, can
be attributed to negligence or inefficiency. On the odd occasion an
archiepiscopal summons to parliament might arrive too late to be
properly executed.[51] But such instances, which may or may not
have resulted in absences, were probably rare, especially in the
more important dioceses. More than anything else the absence of
the lower clergy seems to have stemmed from the determined
defence of clerical privilege, and the use of that privilege to delay
consent to taxation, or to avoid completely consent in parliament.
Before the reign of Edward III attendance of the clerical representatives perhaps fell little short of the attendance of the lay representatives. If, thereafter, it dwindled somewhat in parliaments, there is
every reason to believe that it remained constant and regular in
convocations.

[49] Above p. 2 n. 4 and p. 12 n. 44.
[50] Above pp. 22—3. And see Clarke, *Representation*, esp. pp. 145—50.
[51] *Reg. Martival*, II. ii. 541—2, 579.

4

Expenses

Although there were some proxies of the lower clergy already in print,[1] it was not because of them that twentieth-century historians were made aware of the presence in parliament during the fourteenth century of representatives of the parish clergy. It was rather because of references to the payment of expenses for the clergy's proctors in manorial accounts. These accounts included items of expenditure from the income of churches since the owners of the manors were also the rectors-impropriate of the churches. A reference, in rolls edited in 1895, to a payment from the church of Wootton, Hampshire, in 1338 ('in solutis procuratori existenti pro clero ad parliamentum domini regis, xv *d*') was noted in an article by A. E. Levett in 1927, along with an item from the manorial accounts of Gamlingay, Cambridgeshire. Levett was puzzled: 'How far this was part of a general system I cannot ascertain.' The sequence of references from the Gamlingay accounts was discussed and tabulated by E. C. Lowry in 1933, and further payments were noted by F. M. Page in 1934, from Oakington, Cambridgeshire, and from Langtoft and Baston, Lincolnshire, and by M. Morgan in 1946, from Combe, Berkshire.[2] In a note added to Lowry's important article, A. E. Levett had written in 1933: 'It seems likely that liability to contribute towards the expenses of clerical proctors rested upon rectories and the estates of monastic houses, but . . . it would be interesting to know when and why the detailed assignments were made.' Liability certainly rested upon the rectories (and

---

[1] From diocesan clergy (as well as from cathedral chapters): above p. 11 n. 43 and Wake, *State of the Church*, app. p. 31.

[2] *The Manor of Manydown*, ed. G. W. Kitchin (Hampshire Record Soc., 1895), p. 149, A. E. Levett, 'The financial organisation of the manor', *Economic History Review*, 1 (1927–8), 70, Lowry, 'Clerical proctors', pp. 443–55, Page, *Estates of Crowland*, p. 63 and Morgan, *Lands of Bec*, p. 58 n. 5 (all cited in McHardy, 'Representation of clergy', p. 99).

vicarages), though not upon the temporal income of the monasteries; and information about the 'when and why' can now, in some measure, be provided.

Just as the diocesan clergy elected their representatives in obedience to episcopal writs, so too did they pay for the expenses of their representatives; and the payment of expenses, or, as it was sometimes called, of a 'salarium', like the procedure of elections, was apparently exactly the same for parliaments as for ecclesiastical councils. Several entries in episcopal registers show that bishops, as we would expect, had authority over the collection of the payments. In August 1307 the bishop of Winchester, Henry Woodlock, ordered his archdeacon of Winchester to levy ¼d in the mark from the income of the ecclesiastical persons subject to him to cover the expenses incurred by the proctors at the Carlisle parliament which had lasted for twelve weeks from 20 January. He specifically reserved to himself the authority to increase or decrease the levy. In September he ordered that the payments be raised to 1d in the mark, and, following complaints, decided that the sum collected be used to cover the expenses of the proctors to be sent to the Northampton parliament in October.[3] In April 1313 Bishop Kellaw of Durham intervened, for reasons unstated, to prevent the exaction of a payment, for the expenses of proctors to parliament, from the abbot of St Mary's York apparently in respect of the church of Gainford, in the deanery of Darlington, of which the abbot was rector.[4] In September 1321 Rigaud of Assier, bishop of Winchester, ordered the rural deans in the archdeaconry of Winchester to collect the salary of the clergy's proctor in parliament, as had been agreed;[5] and Bishop Grandisson of Exeter made a similar demand in October 1334 to his archdeacons for payments for proctors to a recent ecclesiastical council.[6]

But the levying of these taxes on the income of the clergy was not a simple matter of the issuing and obeying of episcopal orders. In some dioceses the payment of expenses was agreed upon — and on occasion actually made — at the time of the election of the proctors. When the clergy of the archdeaconry of Winchester chose their proctor in 1321, they decided at the same time upon the salary to be

---

[3] *Reg. Woodlock*, pp. 194−5, 206−7. We learn that the clerical proctors had been required to stay at Carlisle for twelve weeks in LAO, Reg. III (Dalderby), fo. 121v.

[4] *Reg. Kellawe*, I. 310.

[5] *Reg. Asserio*, pp. 424−5.

[6] *Reg. Grandisson*, p. 766, and see p. 1210.

paid to him for his work. In 1307 the clergy of the same arch-deaconry had been required by the bishop to discuss expenses when they elected their proctor for the October parliament and to elect a proctor who would be satisfied with the money available.[7] And, also in 1307, Bishop Dalderby of Lincoln, in the letter ordering his archdeacons to initiate the procedure for the election of proctors for the October parliament, instructed them to avoid a new imposi-tion and to use the apparently large surplus which remained from the money collected for the proctors' expenses for the Carlisle parliament.[8] In his order to the archdeacons for the election of proctors for the parliament of April 1309, Dalderby instructed that the elected proctors should be able to set out immediately for the parliament with their expenses provided by the clergy.[9] And for the parliament of August and December 1311 in London, and for the ecclesiastical council of April 1312 at St Paul's, the bishop again in-cluded in his mandate for the election instructions concerning the provision of expenses; his intention was once again to prevent another levy if there was enough money left over.[10] In 1312 he pointed out to his archdeacons that there was no need in any case to levy more than $\frac{1}{4}d$ in the mark, for this tax was sufficient to provide for the expenses of many proctors assigned to greater business than the current business and in a more distant place. Although the bishop of Lincoln was thus exercising a general super-visory rôle, the immediate responsibility for collection and pay-ment of the proctors was delegated to the archdeacons. And from the mandate of the official of the archdeacon of Northampton to all the rural deans of the archdeaconry concerning the election of proc-tors for the January ecclesiastical council at Lincoln in 1323, it appears that the custom was for the representative from each rural deanery to bring with him the money from the rural deanery which would go to the expenses of the proctors.[11] The surviving episcopal

---

[7] *Reg. Asserio*, pp. 424—5 and *Reg. Woodlock*, p. 207. The Ely clergy agreed to pay $\frac{1}{2}d$ in the mark at the time of the election of their proctors for the ecclesiastical council of Nov. 1377: Aston, *Arundel*, p. 409.

[8] LAO, Reg. III (Dalderby), fo. 121v (transcribed in part in Wake, *State of the Church*, p. 258 n. 7 and thence Weske, *Convocation*, p. 114 n. 134).

[9] LAO, Reg. III (Dalderby), fo. 151r.

[10] *Ibid.*, fos. 221r, 234v, 250r and *Councils and Synods II*, pp. 1363—4.

[11] BL, Cotton Vesp. E xxi, fo. 51v ('precaventes quod quilibet procurator pro vestris decanatibus mittendus secum deferat pecuniam pro-curatoribus ad dictam convocationem Linc' pro clero mittendis, pro sumptibus suis ibidem faciendis, prout moris est, liberandam.').

mandates for the collection of levies were, as we have seen, for expenses already incurred by the proctors; but some proctors plainly carried with them an allowance for their expenses as they set out for parliament.

The levies were on the income of the beneficed clergy, the clergy's spiritual income, as assessed in 1291,[12] and the taxes ranged from ¼d in the mark to 2d in the mark, depending on particular requirements and, of course, on the total spiritual income of each archdeaconry or diocese.[13] The tax in the archdeaconry of Durham for the proctor sent to the parliament of November 1330 was apparently 1d in the pound from the churches of the archdeaconry, which would have raised a total of £5-4s-5d, based upon the revised assessment of the northern province in 1318.[14] In the diocese of Lincoln ¼d in the mark raised, as the bishop pointed out in 1312, a sum which exceeded normal requirements — in fact, a little over £45. The bishop of Winchester in 1307 accepted that 1d in the mark would raise at least £40 in the diocese — indeed, if there was a full response to the levy, the sum would have been £41-3s-2d. That uniform levies within archdeaconries and dioceses were actually being collected can be demonstrated from the evidence. For example, the levy ordered by the bishop of Winchester for the proctor from the archdeaconry of Winchester, who had attended the Carlisle parliament, had been ¼d in the mark, and manorial accounts show that the church of Combe, in the archdeaconry of Winchester, paid 5d, which, since the church was assessed at 20 marks, represents ¼d in the mark.[15] And we have the record of payments from two churches in the diocese of Ely for proctors sent to an ecclesiastical council in 1302 and to the parliament at York in May 1322: on both occasions, 13d from the church of Oakington, assessed at 26 marks, and 8¾d from the moiety of the church of Gamlingay, the whole church having been assessed at 35 marks.[16]

---

[12] As is made clear in *Reg. Woodlock*, p. 195 and *Reg. Grandisson*, p. 766.

[13] The totals of each diocese from the 1291 assessment as printed in *Taxatio* are conveniently listed in W. Stubbs, *The Constitutional History of England*, II (Oxford, 1896), table facing p. 580. And see *Reg. Martival*, I. 429−31 and *Reg. Hethe*, p. 51.

[14] Appendix 3, and, for the assessed spiritualities of the archdeaconry of Durham, see *Taxatio*, pp. 329−30.

[15] *Reg. Woodlock*, p. 194, Morgan, *Lands of Bec*, p. 58 n. 5 and *Taxatio*, p. 212b.

[16] Page, *Estates of Crowland*, p. 63, Lowry, 'Clerical proctors', pp. 448−9 and *Taxatio*, pp. 265b, 266b. For the acquisition of the moiety of Gamlingay by Merton College, Oxford, see *Early Rolls of Merton*, ed. Highfield, p. 45.

The levy in the diocese of Ely in 1302 and again in 1322 was thus ½d in the mark, which would have raised on each occasion £9-4s-1d. Even so, the list of payments from the church of Gamlingay, running from 1280 to 1374, are rather puzzling since they do not always correspond to a simple fraction in the mark or in the pound.[17]

From all this evidence it is not possible to deduce the actual amounts paid to each proctor. There are too many complicating factors: a single levy was often used for more than one assembly; it is rarely clear how many proctors were actually being paid; and who would be responsible for paying a multiple capacity proctor? Paying the proctor of the diocesan clergy was largely an *ad hoc* affair, as was also the paying of the proctors from cathedral chapters. Each chapter had to agree to the rate of pay and give its consent to a period of absence of the proctor. The proctor was often himself a member of the chapter, and it had to be determined whether he would be granted the usual allowance from the common fund while he was non-resident.[18] The expenses depended on the status, and therefore the size of the entourage, of the chosen representative. When the treasurer of Lincoln was elected to represent the chapter of Lincoln at the ecclesiastical council of November 1309 in London he said that he could not travel with less than ten horses, that in winter time six days had to be allowed for getting to London and six days for getting back, and that although prices were higher than usual he would be content with 1s a day for each horse. Thus he required £6 just for the travelling expenses. And when the subprior of Durham and the bursar of Durham attended convocations at York, they were paid respectively £2-3s-3d for six days (7s-2½d a day) and £3-8s-9d for eleven days (6s-3d a day).[19] But one of the proctors of the chapter of Worcester who attended

---

[17] Lowry, 'Clerical proctors', pp. 448—53. Eight out of 22 of the recorded payments from the moiety of Gamlingay after the 1291 assessment do represent a fraction of the assessed value of 17½ marks (½d in the pound in 1294, 1295, 1296 and 1342, ½d in the mark in 1302 and 1322, 2d in the mark in 1307, and ¼d in the mark in 1327). But other payments must be based upon a changed assessment of the moiety of the church: certainly in 1318—19, 1322—3 and 1334 the levy was upon an assessment at 17 marks rather than 17½ marks.

[18] *Councils and Synods II*, p. 1252, and see W. Nigel Yates, 'John of Ross and a dispute over commons, 1317—24', *BIHR*, 48 (1975), 16—21.

[19] *Councils and Synods II*, p. 1252 and *Extracts from the Account Rolls of the Abbey of Durham*, ed. J. T. Fowler (Surtees Soc., 1898—1901), II. 576 and III. 594 (for the years of accounts 1370—1 and 1384—5).

the parliament at York in September 1314 was paid the more modest sum of 40s; and the itemised expenses of the warden of Merton College, Oxford, and two fellows of the College and others with them, who spent four weeks at the parliament in London of March 1300, came to a total of £3-18s-10¼d, which included 14s for the rent of rooms.[20]

In the writs 'de expensis' of early 1327 and thereafter the rates of pay for the burgesses and for the knights were fixed at, respectively, 2s a day and 4s a day.[21] The proctors of the clergy were perhaps paid on average something between these two rates. But there was, no doubt, so much variation in practice — as probably also, in fact, for the knights and certainly for the burgesses[22] — that there is little point in guessing at an average rate of pay. It is no surprise that the clergy never obtained writs 'de expensis' with which to bolster and verify their expense accounts, for writs enjoining payments would have been tantamount to admitting that they could be required by the Crown to attend. There may well often have been delay in the payment of full expenses to the clerical proctors, and those responsible for collecting the levies may have been in the habit of taking a cut.[23] But there is nothing to suggest that the cumbersome method of paying for the work of the clerical representatives did not, in general, work quite smoothly. It was of necessity cumbersome, since each beneficed churchman who was represented in parliament not only took part in the election of his representatives but also paid for their work. The spiritual income of the clergy was, of course, derived in the main from the tithes of the produce of the inhabitants of each parish. Yet it is of crucial significance that it was not in any strict sense those inhabitants who paid the clerical proctors. The constituents of the clerical proctors were without any question the clergy themselves.

---

[20] See below p. 109 n. 31, and *Early Rolls of Merton*, ed. Highfield, pp. 338–9, 341–2.
[21] *Parl. Writs*, II. ii. 364–5, and see Cam, 'Community of the shire', p. 237.
[22] McKisack, *Representation of Boroughs*, pp. 82–99.
[23] See esp. *Reg. Woodlock*, pp. 194–5, 206–7 and *Councils and Synods II*, pp. 1363–4.

5

Political Influence

Much of the discussion in previous chapters strongly indicates the capacity of the cathedral clergy and diocesan clergy to organise themselves so that their voice could be heard. Their letters of proxy will provide us with some information for an assessment of the influence which they exercised especially in defence of their rights. But we must begin by looking at other evidence. The exertion of political pressure by the lower clergy, in particular the diocesan clergy, through their representatives as well as through the ecclesiastical hierarchy, is firmly attested in the sources. F. M. Powicke underestimated the corporate sense of the lower clergy.[1] Indeed, there is much direct evidence, from the thirteenth and early fourteenth centuries, of the influence, or attempted influence, upon the Crown of the representatives of the clergy — more, for this period, than of the influence of the knights of the shire and the burgesses.

We shall consider first the activities of the lower clergy within the Church itself. It is clear that groups of them, whether from rural deaneries or cities or dioceses, could and often did act corporately. For example, in 1281 or thereabouts, the rectors, vicars and parish priests of the deanery of Holderness complained to the archbishop of York, that when the archdeacon's official came to hold rural chapters he brought with him a greatly increased retinue, including the archbishop's sequestrator and an apparitor recently inflicted upon them by the archbishop's official, amounting to a total of eight or nine mounts, compared with only three or four in the past. In 1309 the rectors and 'curati' of the city of London set down in a detailed list their grievances against the friars, in order to present the complaints as a petition to the bishops of the province. And the clergy of the diocese of Carlisle protested to their bishop, in a letter

---

[1] F. M. Powicke, *Thirteenth Century* (Oxford, 2nd edn 1961) pp. 448—9 (though the comments here should be studied along with the analysis on pp. 497—507).

preserved among others dated 1338 in the bishop's register, that he was collecting procurations from clerical income using the wrong taxation assessment.[2] Moreover it is evident that at times the archbishop of Canterbury instructed his bishops to collect grievances from the clergy for the reform of the Church. The petition of the London clergy in 1309 may well have been in response to specific instructions from Archbishop Winchelsey (himself reacting to Clement V's 'Regnans in celis') that there should be local inquiries concerning those matters needing reform. We know that the bishop of Winchester made arrangements for deliberations with the clergy of his diocese.[3] In 1328 Archbishop Mepham ordered that his bishops, before setting out for the ecclesiastical council of January 1329, should initiate inquiries with the clergy of their dioceses concerning any deficiencies or grievances which should be dealt with in the council. The complaints of the clergy of the diocese of Exeter are preserved in Bishop Grandisson's register; and in the diocese of Salisbury the clergy of each archdeaconry were required to decide upon the deficiencies and grievances needing reform and redress and the proctor of each archdeaconry was charged to bring this information to the meeting at Salisbury at which the proctors to represent the whole diocese were to be chosen. Bishop Martival directed that discussion should take place at this meeting to determine which matters were to be taken forward to the council, to be proposed there by the bishop or by the clergy's proctors.[4]

As for the clerical *gravamina* against the operations of the king's courts,[5] the general procedure appears to have been for the formulation of the articles of complaint in ecclesiastical councils, following consultations with the clergy, and the presentation of the articles by the bishops to the king and council in parliament. But we should not imagine that the proctors of the lower clergy never themselves presented petitions in parliament. In a list of those presented at the Michaelmas parliament of 1318[6] we find, among many individual petitions and some from burgesses and county 'communities', the following from the clergy: 'Due petitiones pro

2   *Reg. Wickwane*, pp. 248−9 (translated in Moorman, *Church Life*, p. 122); *Councils and Synods II*, pp. 1255−63; and CRO, Reg. Kirkby, p. 372.

3   *Councils and Synods II*, pp. 1241−2, 1266−8. And see Denton, 'Clergy and parliament', pp. 97−9.

4   *Concilia*, II. 548−9, *Reg. Grandisson*, pp. 446−8 and *Reg. Martival*, II. ii. 596.

5   Jones, '*Gravamina* of the clergy'.

6   *Rot. Parl. Inediti*, pp. 78−80.

clero regni de prohibitione', 'Petitio de corrodiis concessis per regem in diversis locis et abbatiis qui (sic) non debent onerari',[7] 'Petitio religiosorum de archiepiscopatu Eboracensi', 'Canonici Karliolenses', 'Pro beneficiatis pauperibus', and 'Communitas cleri aliquando plur[alis]'. It is more than likely that the elected proctors of the cathedral and diocesan clergy had a hand in formulating and in presenting at least some of these clerical petitions. In a petition of uncertain date, but apparently from the reign of either Edward I or Edward II, the 'parsons' of Holderness complained that tithes were not being paid from the king's mills in Holderness; and the beneficed clergy of the archdeaconry of Stow and the clergy of the diocese of York petitioned in the parliaments of January 1315 and November 1325 concerning their respective assessments for taxation.[8]

There can be no doubt whatever that taxation was the issue which affected the lower clergy more than any other. The reason for their deep concern is not hard to find. Their income was not from estates. It was in no sense temporal. It was income for the cure of souls. And when the English Church was taxed, whether by pope or by king, only one third of the proceeds came from the temporal income of the bishops and monasteries.[9] The rest came from the spiritual income of the beneficed clergy. We can hardly be surprised at evidence of the anger of the lower clergy against their bishops, who were often on the side of authority. Simon of Ghent, bishop of Salisbury, in 1310 explained in a letter to Edward II that the clergy protested bitterly to the prelates about the heavy demands imposed upon them.[10] Indeed, there are many sets of complaints from the lower clergy about taxation. By 1295 there was already a long tradition of the clergy's proctors presenting grievances about financial demands from popes and kings. The rectors of the archdeaconry of Berkshire had protested in 1240 against papal demands for a subsidy, drawing up a list of eighteen reasons why they ought not to contribute; proctors of the English clergy had formulated their complaints in 1246 against papal exactions; in 1254 the 'nuntii' of the chapters, colleges and clergy of England had agreed to the deflection to the war in Gascony of money granted to

---

[7] This complaint had been answered, apparently unsatisfactorily, in the *Articuli Cleri* of 1316: see *Statutes*, I. 173.

[8] *Rot. Parl.*, I. 314, 433, 474. The answer to the petition from the archdeaconry of Stow is in PRO E159/88 m. 30v.

[9] See above p. 57 n. 13.

[10] *Reg. Gandavo*, p. 395, cited in Clarke, *Representation*, p. 334.

the pope for a crusade on conditions which were so demanding that their response amounted to a refusal; in 1256 articles of complaint against the policies of the king and against papal taxation had apparently been drawn up in every diocese of the realm by proctors of the beneficed clergy, and the annalist of Burton has preserved for us the detailed list of grievances of the proctors of the archdeaconry of Lincoln and of the diocese of Coventry and Lichfield; in 1269 the proctors of the abbots, priors, rectors and vicars of nineteen of the dioceses of England and Wales — excluding only Bangor and St Asaph — had presented their reasons for refusing to grant a royal subsidy; and in 1276 complaints against papal taxes and allegations against the papal collectors had been set down by the clergy of the diocese of Salisbury and are preserved in the register of the bishop of Winchester.[11] After 1295 the proctors of the clergy continued to present complaints about taxation. It must be stressed, however, that the grievances which have survived, for 1296—7, 1314—15 and 1323, were addressed to the bishops of the province or to the archbishop of Canterbury and were associated with the work of the proctors in ecclesiastical councils rather than in parliaments.[12] Nevertheless, they demonstrate what must have been, on many occasions, the most important matter of concern to the men elected in response to the royal summonses.

The lower clergy were able to protest when royal subsidies were requested, and were able to attempt to impose conditions, because the principle of consent to taxation upon spiritualities was firmly established.[13] When the king tried to impose a subsidy the lower clergy, unlike the laity, could and often did both object and

[11] *Councils and Synods II*, pp. 288—92, for 1240 (and see Lunt, *Financial Relations to 1327*, pp. 201—2 and Smith, *Church and State*, pp. 25—9); *Councils and Synods II*, pp. 398—401, for 1246; *ibid.*, pp. 482—3, for 1254 (and see Lunt, 'Consent of lower clergy', pp. 140—4 and Clarke, *Representation*, p. 309); *Councils and Synods II*, pp. 506—9, for 1256 (and see Lunt, 'Consent of lower clergy', pp. 145—7 and Lunt, *Financial Relations to 1327*, pp. 270—1); *Councils and Synods II*, pp. 798—800, for 1269 (and see Lunt, 'Consent of lower clergy', pp. 160—1 and Clarke, *Representation*, p. 310); and *Reg. Pontissara*, pp. 362—4, for 1276 (and see *Councils and Synods II*, p. 816 n. 1).

[12] *Councils and Synods II*, pp. 1156—7, for 1296—7 (and see Denton, *Winchelsey*, pp. 102—3); *Parl. Writs*, II. ii. 123—4, 139, and app. p. 92, and Denton 'Communitas cleri', pp. 76—8, for 1314—16 (and see Denton, 'Reynolds and ecclesiastical politics', pp. 258—74); and *Concilia*, II. 517—19, for 1323.

[13] See esp. Lunt, 'Consent of lower clergy'.

refuse. Strong opposition to taxation came, for example, from the lower clergy of the southern province in 1295—6 and from the lower clergy of the northern province in 1311.[14] And, long before it was possible for the laity, when the clergy agreed to a subsidy they could make efforts to control the supply of money: as in 1254 when their grant was conditional upon the king invading Gascony and as in 1297 when the condition of full payment of a subsidy was the continuing needs of the king.[15] For the parish clergy there can be no doubt whatever that it was primarily the right to consent to taxation which led to the need for proper representation in assemblies. There are firm indications in the middle years of the thirteenth century that the archdeacons were still regarded as representing the interests of the parish clergy; but their authoritative and official status meant that they could not act effectively as the clergy's representatives. Maude Clarke summed up the position: 'The assumption of identity of interest between either the bishop or the archdeacon and the lower clergy simply broke down under the financial strain, and it became necessary to devise a new plan of representation.'[16]

The procedures which emerged were not just a matter of the election of proctors. The representatives may have required their instructions,[17] and for this purpose discussion at times took place in diocesan assemblies prior to ecclesiastical councils. Taxation was discussed in diocesan assemblies in the critical years 1283 and 1294.[18] And on some occasions there might well have been a need formally to report back to the diocesan clergy the decisions which had been taken. Henry of Eastry, prior of Canterbury, as keeper of spiritualities *sede vacante*, wrote to the archdeacon of Canterbury on 2 October 1294, following the ecclesiastical gathering of 21 September summoned by the king. He recalled the diocesan meeting at which two proctors had been appointed, and he instructed the archdeacon to summon another diocesan assembly for 6 October of all the abbots and priors, especially those with

[14] *Councils and Synods II*, pp. 1156—7, 1340—1.
[15] Clarke, *Representation*, p. 309 and Denton, *Winchelsey*, pp. 173—4, 189, 213. And see G. L. Harriss, 'Parliamentary taxation and the origins of appropriation of supply in England, 1207—1340', *Recueils de la Société Jean Bodin*, 24 (1966), 167—79.
[16] Clarke, *Representation*, p. 307 and Denton, 'Clergy and parliament', p. 96.
[17] Concerning instructions to proctors see Post, '*Plena potestas* and consent', pp. 133—8, 147—9.
[18] *Councils and Synods II*, pp. 947, 1128—9.

appropriated churches, and all the beneficed clergy so that they could be informed as quickly as possible of what had been decided by the clergy of the realm.[19] The news was certainly important, for the enormous tax of a half of the clergy's income had been conceded. In later years attempts were made actually to obtain consent from the separate meetings in the dioceses. These meetings probably became more representative than the traditional diocesan synods, and many clergy perhaps attended by proxy.[20] In summoning an ecclesiastical council to meet on 9 June 1322 Archbishop Reynolds related how it had not been possible to obtain full consent to a tax of 5d in the mark at the York parliament of 2 May because of the absence of some clergy including the clerical proctors from certain dioceses. Bishops were instructed to summon meetings of their clergy and, if consent could be obtained, to proceed with the collection of the tax. Only when consent was not forthcoming was attendance at the ecclesiastical council required. In the Salisbury diocese the clerical meetings appear to have taken place in the archdeaconries and the decisions brought to Salisbury by a proctor elected in each archdeaconry. Because of the nature of the business abbots and priors of the diocese, as well as secular clergy, had been summoned to give their consent, and all did so except a few exempt abbots and priors, whose names were notified to the archbishop.[21] Diocesan assemblies were once again ordered, by the king, in 1337, 1339 and 1340.[22]

---

[19] CUL, Ee. v. 31, fo. 62v (in *Concilia*, II. 201−2).

[20] See C. R. Cheney, *English Synodalia of the Thirteenth Century* (Oxford, reprinted 1968), p. 4. For the proxy of the subprior and convent of Bath, dated 23 Nov. 1342, for a convocation of clergy summoned to meet before the bishop of Bath and Wells at Taunton on 27 Nov. 1342 see LI, Hale 185, fo. 165.

[21] *Parl. Writs*, II. ii. 259 (and *Concilia*, II. 515−16), and *Reg. Martival*, II. ii. 395−8. And see Clarke, *Representation*, p. 144 n. 3. For the *forma* of the tax of 5d in the mark see BL, Cotton Vesp. E xxi, fo. 49.

[22] For Sept. 1337 see *Foedera*, II. ii. 990 and *Dignity of a Peer*, IV. 485, *Reg. Grandisson*, I. 301−2, EDR, Reg. Montacute, fos. 69r−70r, HWRO, Reg. Hempnall, pp. 68−9 (in Wake, *State of the Church*, app. p. 62), E. Hobhouse, 'Register of Roger de Norbury', *William Salt Archaeological Soc.*, old ser. 1 (1880), 268, 270, J. F. Willard, 'Edward III's negotiations for a grant in 1337', *EHR*, 21 (1906), 728, 730−1, and Clarke, *Representation*, p. 149; and for 1339 and 1340 see *Concilia*, II. 654−5, 659, *Reg. Shrewsbury*, pp. 357, 380, and Kemp, *Counsel and Consent*, p. 102 (citing H. E. Reynolds, *Wells Cathedral* (1881), p. 151 where Wells, D. & C. Muniments, Liber Ruber, fo. 57v is printed).

In all this representation and discussion we must not imagine that the clergy were interested only in defending their incomes, without a care for the interests of the realm. Taxation could not be debated without consideration of either papal or royal policies. The Berkshire rectors in 1240 had given their opinions of the relations between the pope and emperor and between England and the emperor, and they had compared the position of the English clergy with that of the French clergy. The complaints of the proctors of the archdeaconry of Lincoln and of the diocese of Coventry and Lichfield in 1256 had been drawn up specifically 'pro communitate'.[23] In the parliament of January 1315 the clergy granted a tenth to the king and attached conditions to their grant. These included not only the provision that ecclesiastical liberties be restored but also that peace should be established between the king and the magnates, that the Ordinances of 1311 should be observed and that all concessions against the terms of the Ordinances should be revoked.[24] In the unusual ecclesiastical council of 1 December 1321, attended by magnates and officials who were loyal to the king, the proctors of the lower clergy played their part in deciding that the process against the Despensers should be revoked.[25] The clergy of the Canterbury province refused a tax in January 1323 and in so doing they challenged their archbishop to speak openly to the king and to the leaders of the kingdom and to present them with the reasons for their failure against the Scots: the clergy's petition was an eloquent and bitter attack upon what they regarded as the sacrilegious and perfidious behaviour of the English magnates.[26]

When the proxies themselves referred to the nature of the business to be dealt with in a forthcoming parliament they were echoing the terms of the writs of summons: see, for examples, the proxy of the clergy of the Lincoln diocese for the Carlisle parliament of 1307 'super ordinatione et stabilimento terre Scotie', the proxy of the clergy of the archdeaconry of Shropshire for the Northampton parliament later in the year 'pro humatione corporis pie memorie domini Edwardi quondam regis Anglie ac solempnitate sponsalium et coronationis dicti domini Edwardi regis nunc regnantis', and the proxy of the Durham chapter for the parliament of September 1327 'super defensione et custodia regni Anglie'.[27] But,

23 Above p. 63 n. 11.
24 *Parl. Writs*, II. ii. app. 92 and *Reg. Swinfield*, pp. 497–8. And see Denton, 'Reynolds and ecclesiastical politics', pp. 260–1.
25 Clarke, *Representation*, pp. 138, 168–70.
26 *Concilia*, II. 517–19 and *Parl. Writs*, II. ii. 283–4.
27 LAO, Reg. III (Dalderby), fo. 108v and *Parl. Writs*, I. ii. 182; PRO

all the same, it is difficult to believe that the summons of the clergy
to give consent to decisions on what were often weighty matters of
policy, and the consequent grant by the clergy to proctors of the
right to give consent, were mere formalities. There must have been
some procedure whereby the clergy's proctors gave consent to
those matters ordained at parliaments. They had been summoned
to do so and were empowered to do so. We know next to nothing
of this process, even when, as was so often the case, taxation was at
issue. This silence suggests, not only that a record of these important proceedings was considered unnecessary, but also that the proceedings generally caused little open friction or excitement, which
would have attracted the attention of chroniclers. The clerical proctors would not have remained at the parliaments if they had
nothing to do. They stayed at the last parliament of Edward I at
Carlisle for twelve weeks.[28] This was, it is true, a parliament at
which ecclesiastical matters figured large. An instructive, if
negative, report from the bishop of Salisbury survives concerning
the parliament of December 1311. Archbishop Winchelsey had
given as the reason for his summons of the clergy to this parliament
the arduous and diverse business concerning the state of the king
and the needs of the kingdom. But the bishop of Salisbury reported
that, although the clergy who had arrived were prepared to give
their consent to the matters to be ordained, no parliament in fact
took place for them ('parliamentum aliquod tunc eis minime
apparebat'). Instead, there had been two weeks of secret discus-
sions between certain prelates and magnates to which the clergy
had not been admitted, and so they had gone back home, some
because of tedium and others because of lack of finances, without
accomplishing the business for which they had come ('infecto pro
quo venerant negotio').[29] The clergy could sometimes be ignored,
but they did not expect to be ignored.

The proxies tell us nothing about the nature of parliamentary
'negotia', but they do provide evidence that the right of the clerical
proctors to give consent should not be interpreted as acceptance by
the clergy of submission to the royal will. Representatives were
summoned to consent to decisions already reached or to be
reached. The clause of guarantee in the proxies, which declared
that the constituents in the chapter and diocese would hold 'ratum

---

SC10/1/28 (see Appendix 1(b)) and *Parl. Writs*, II. ii. 1; and
SC10/11/518 and *Dignity of a Peer*, IV. 376.

[28] LAO, Reg. III (Dalderby), fo. 121v.

[29] *Reg. Gandavo*, pp. 410, 418.

et gratum' whatever the proctors did, constituted ratification in advance. The necessity of further consultation with the constituents was precluded. This is the undisputed force of the vast majority of the surviving capitular and diocesan proxies. We can learn more, however, from some important exceptions. It has already been noted that proctors were, perhaps as a matter of course, issued with duplicate proxies,[30] and the proxies of Bishop Dalderby of Lincoln, appointing personal proctors, demonstrate that two or more proxies drawn up for a parliament could sometimes differ in essential elements. The entries in Dalderby's register show that he was in the habit of giving his proctors two proxies, one openly addressed and the other addressed to the king, as for the Carlisle parliament of 1307 and for the parliament of February 1309.[31] He did the same for the parliament of April 1309, but then also sent a third which included an additional clause. This was the all-important clause 'to do and to consent to those matters to be ordained there' and he instructed his proctor to use this last proxy if it proved necessary, but otherwise not at all.[32] The alternative forms of proxy were provided again for the autumn parliament of 1311, the parliaments of August 1312 and July 1313, the ecclesiastical council, summoned by the king, of May 1314, and also for the parliament of January 1316, on which last occasion the proxy, addressed to the king, which was presented at parliament and which thus survives in the Public Record Office, was a proxy in the weaker form, without the consenting clause.[33]

Bishop Dalderby wanted to give restricted powers to his proctors. The Lincoln chapter also on occasion gave its proctors differently worded warrants. For the ecclesiastical council of 1309 the chapter drew up two proxies, and the one which they said should be used, if possible, omitted the word 'obedientia' in the address to the archbishop.[34] But especially interesting are the different proxies drawn up by the chapter of Lincoln for the parliament of November 1325.[35] The chapter's two representatives were given three proxies, the first described as 'more limiting than the others',

---

[30] Above pp. 35—6.
[31] LAO, Reg. III (Dalderby), fos. 110v, 148v—149r.
[32] *Ibid.*, fo 153v: 'Ita quod uteretur illo procuratorio si necesse foret alioquin nullo modo.'
[33] *Ibid.*, fos. 235r, 259r—260r, 277r, 296r—297v, 337v and PRO SC10/4/196.
[34] *Councils and Synods II*, p. 1252.
[35] See Appendix 2. For a similar example of the chapter of Rheims issuing different proxies see Brown, 'Representation and agency law', p. 331.

the second as 'a little bit limiting' and the third as 'more general'. It was made plain that the first was preferred, that the second could be used if there was no way of avoiding it and the third should only be used if it was absolutely necessary. The preferred proxy included two notable clauses: the first stated that the proctors were to consent to what was ordained in so far as the chapter was able and ought to be lawfully bound to do those things ('quatenus ad ista facienda de iure artari poterimus et debemus'); and the second clause, even more unusual, was a provision that the proctors should agree to no contribution towards a subsidy without prior consultation with the chapter ('proviso quod iidem procuratores vel eorum alter nulli contributioni faciende nobis consentiant vel consentiat inconsultis'). The second proxy excluded the latter of these two clauses but maintained the former. The third proxy excluded both clauses. So it was only this third proxy which provided full ratification in advance. We do not know which proxy was used, for no original from the Lincoln chapter is extant for this parliament.

These three proxies drawn up by the Lincoln chapter show that the clerical proctors in parliament had a power which might be regarded as too great for comfort. The first of the proxies, requiring consultation about taxation, is exceptional, but some other proxies which were presented in parliament are similar in wording to the second proxy and may well amount to deliberate limitations of the powers of the proctors. The proxy of the clergy of the Durham diocese for the Northampton parliament of 1307 declared that the proctors should do what was required by law and by custom ('que de iure et consuetudine requiruntur'), and the proxy of the clergy of the archdeaconry of Northumberland in November 1330 gave their proctor the right to do all those things which were necessary or opportune ('que necessaria fuerit vel oportuna').[36] Qualifications were sometimes even incorporated into the 'ratum et gratum' clause, thus declaring that the constituents would hold firm to what the proctors do within reason ('rationabiliter') or in so far as they were able and were bound by law ('quantum ad nos pertinet et de iure tenemur').[37]

A few other proxies, from the northern clergy, included clauses which appear to have been designed to ensure that the proctors were able to act according to the constituents' instructions. Instead of simply granting their proctor the right to give consent, the clergy

---

[36] PRO SC10/1/38, /14/696.
[37] SC10/2/93, /15/720, /16/788, /17/849.

of the archdeaconry of Durham in 1318 stated that he should be present in parliament 'to give consent or to refuse to give consent to the things done as should seem to be expedient' ('ad consentiendum seu contradicendum hiis que ibidem gesta fuerint prout melius videbitur expedire'). Similarly, the same clergy in February 1334 and in 1335 and the clergy of the archdeaconry of Northumberland in February 1334 and March 1336 granted their proctors the right 'to dissent wherever, as often as ever and whenever it was necessary and should seem to them to be expedient for us' ('et ad dissentiendum ubicumque quotienscumque et quandocumque opus fuerit et sibi videbitur pro nobis expedire').[38] These clauses are surely linked with the clergy's reluctance to grant taxes in parliament and with their reluctance, at times, as we have seen,[39] to send any proctors at all to parliament. The fear was that the proctors might be put under great pressure to give consent and lose sight of the wishes of their constituents. The clergy were holding firmly to their right to refuse taxation. If they had less of a rôle to play in parliament between 1295 and 1340 than the knights of the shire and the burgesses — which is debatable, especially before 1327 — it was not because they were politically weak, but rather because they had a greater capacity to avoid the direct authority of, and even to defy, royal government.

What of the men who represented the lower clergy in parliament? For the forty-five parliaments between 1295 and March 1340 we have collected 301 names.[40] There is, in general, a clear distinction between those who served chapters and those who served diocesan clergy, but twenty-two men at some stage served both. Many will always remain obscure, though some were men of importance outside their dioceses. It should be noted at the outset that the list of names and titles in Appendix 5 provides information which was not used in the compiling of the revised Le Neve's *Fasti Ecclesiae Anglicanae*, nor by A. B. Emden in his biographical registers of Oxford and Cambridge. The 301 names of proctors are drawn from 430 appointments; in other words, 129 appointments

---

[38] SC10/6/256A, /18/858, /18/870, /18/879, /19/944 (see Appendix 1(k)).

[39] Above pp. 51—2.

[40] This total was arrived at by a careful count, but precision is not in fact possible. For example, is David, archdeacon of Bangor, the same as the earlier David Buellt, canon of Bangor? We have assumed not. Is it the same John de Thoresby who acted for the chapter of Coventry, the York clergy and the clergy of the archdeaconry of Durham? We have assumed so (see Emden, *Oxford*, III. 1863).

were of a man who had already acted as a proctor for the lower clergy in parliament. But it is only possible to begin to judge the frequency of re-appointment if we concentrate on those constituencies with names of proctors for more than say ten out of the forty-five parliaments. We know of more letters of proxy from the chapters than from the parish clergy: 177 compared with eighty-four, figures which include references to proxies which have not survived. And there are only three dioceses for which we know the names of the proctors for more than ten parliaments (York, Durham and Carlisle) compared with seven of the chapters (York, Canterbury, Worcester, St Asaph, Durham and Bangor). Two proctors were more usually appointed for each parliament, but often, from the chapters, only one and sometimes three or four. The rate of re-appointment for these dioceses and chapters is as follows:

York chapter: for twenty parliaments, twenty-five proctors. One appointed eight times (John Giffard, canon of York), one appointed five times (M. Henry de Cliffe, canon of York and royal clerk), one appointed four times, three appointed three times and five appointed twice.

Canterbury chapter: for nineteen parliaments, twenty-four individual proctors. Four appointed twice.

Worcester chapter: for nineteen parliaments, thirteen individual proctors. One appointed eight times and once also for the clergy of the Worcester archdeaconry (Thomas de Evesham, royal clerk), one appointed three times and four appointed twice.

St Asaph chapter: for seventeen parliaments, twelve individual proctors. One appointed six times (M. Richard de Oswaldestre, canon of St Asaph), one appointed four times and three appointed also by the Bangor chapter.

York diocese: for fifteen parliaments, twenty-four individual proctors. One appointed three times and four appointed twice.

Durham chapter: for thirteen parliaments, sixteen individual proctors. One appointed four times, one three times and three twice, and two were appointed also by the Durham clergy.

Bangor chapter: for twelve parliaments, twelve individual proctors. One appointed five times (M. David de Buellt, canon of Bangor), three appointed twice, and three appointed also by the St Asaph chapter.

Ely chapter: for twelve parliaments, fourteen individual proctors. Two appointed three times and four twice.

Durham diocese: for eleven parliaments, seventeen individual proctors. Two appointed twice and three appointed also by other constituencies (Durham chapter and Coventry chapter).

Carlisle diocese: for eleven parliaments, seventeen individual proctors. One appointed five times (M. Adam de Appelby, rector of Caldbeck), one appointed three times and two twice.

In each of these cases the parliaments for which the proctors are known are spread quite evenly across the period. Re-appointments sometimes occurred for consecutive parliaments, but more usually for parliaments within a limited period of up to about ten years. A few proctors served for a longer period: John Giffard was a proctor for the York chapter at least eight times between 1328 and 1340, David de Buellt for the Bangor chapter at least five times between 1313 and 1331, Thomas de Evesham for the Worcester chapter at least eight times between 1314 and 1340, and Richard de Oswaldestre for the St Asaph chapter at least six times between 1313 and 1340. In general, as we would expect, the higher the number of proxies that have survived for a constituency the higher the incidence of re-appointment: thus for both the York chapter and the Worcester chapter fifty per cent of the appointments are re-appointments. Even so, there appears to be an uncommonly high rate of re-appointment by these two chapters and certainly an uncommonly low rate by the Canterbury chapter, seventeen per cent, and by the York diocesan clergy, twenty per cent. All in all, the rate of re-appointment is sufficient to suggest that at most parliaments there was a complement of proctors of the lower clergy with experience of parliamentary procedures.

A large number of the proctors, forty-five per cent, were university-trained, that is they were given the title of master.[41] The percentage should probably be somewhat higher, for the title was

[41] There is no reason to think that in this context the title was merely honorific: see Cheney, *Notaries*, pp. 89—90.

not always included, as we know from the proxies of the re-appointed. A much higher percentage of the parish clergy's proctors, sixty-one per cent, than of the chapters' proctors, thirty-seven per cent, were masters. The percentage of masters sent by chapters is low partly because the monastic cathedral churches most often sent their monks as proctors: only twenty-six per cent of the proctors of the monastic chapters were styled master compared with fifty per cent of the proctors of the secular chapters.

Perhaps between ten and fifteen per cent of the proctors were royal clerks; these were in the main the proctors of secular cathedrals, in which they held prebends.[42] Clearly, both academic training, which was often in canon law and/or civil law,[43] and some experience in the world of ecclesiastical and royal administration were significant qualifications for the proctor. A novice could face difficulties. The point is illustrated by a letter from the prior of Norwich to the dean of the Arches, Richard de Stanhowe, in 1316 about the proctors who had been elected to represent both himself and the chapter of Norwich at the forthcoming ecclesiastical council of 28 April at St Paul's. The prior was especially concerned, it seems, that his absence should be tactfully excused. He asked that one of Richard de Stanhowe's clerks, who was instructed in such matters, should give advice and assistance to the proctors, particularly in presenting their proxies, since they were not adequately informed for executing business of this kind.[44]

[42] See Roskell, 'Consideration of *Modus*', pp. 425—8 (more capitular proxies have survived than are noted here). And for the king's clerks present at Carlisle in 1307 in proctorial capacities see G. P. Cuttino, 'King's clerks and the community of the realm', *Speculum*, 29 (1954), 404 n. 74.

[43] The York clergy appointed a number of men who were described as advocates of the court of York (M. William de Neusom', M. Richard de Wath and M. Thomas de Harpham). M. Philip, archdeacon of St Davids, who acted as a proctor for both the clergy and the chapter of St Davids, was described as a professor of canon law, as also was M. Geoffrey de Pakenham, proctor of the Ely chapter; M. John de Schoredich, proctor of the Bath chapter, as professor of civil law; and M. Richard de Eryum, proctor of the Durham chapter and three times proctor of the York chapter, as professor of both laws. Study of the careers of other proctors would produce more examples: for instance, M. Peter de Medeburn, proctor of the Lincoln clergy, was a doctor of canon law (see Emden, *Oxford*, III. 1251).

[44] Norwich, D. & C. Muniments, Reg. IX, fo. 10r: '. . . rogamus quatinus confratribus nostris, quos pro nobis et capitulo nostro procuratores deputavimus, consilio si placet et auxilio et maxime in procuratoriis

Some of the cathedral clergy's proctors were men of note. Two became bishops of the cathedral churches they had represented (Hamo Hethe, Rochester, in 1309 and March 1313, and Matthew de Englefield, Bangor, in 1324 and February 1328), and the future archbishop of Canterbury, Simon Islip, acted, when he was arch-deacon of Stow, for the Lincoln chapter, in 1332. M. Adam Murimuth, doctor of civil law, royal diplomat, and chronicler, was appointed on 19 April 1319 to represent the chapter of Canterbury at the parliament of York on 6 May 1319. Among other commissions he had already acted for the chapter of Canterbury at the papal court, was in receipt of 60s a year from the chapter and was already a canon of Hereford, Wells and Exeter.[45] But it seems certain that Murimuth cannot in fact have travelled to York to act for the Canterbury monks in 1319. He noted in his chronicle that at a meeting in London immediately after Easter 1319 (an ecclesiastical council met on 20 April, twelve days after Easter) he was sent to the papal court, by the prelates but at the expense of the king, to obtain permission for the clergy to grant a tenth to the king.[46] The pope's favourable reply was dated 29 May. Although Murimuth was thus unable, it appears, to act as proctor in parliament on this occasion, the fact that he had been named by the monks at Canterbury suggests a question: is there any reason to believe that the chroniclers of this period presented a viewpoint which coincided with that of the lower clergy?

During the first half of the fourteenth century there was a marked increase in the proportion of chronicles that were written by secular clerks. They do not, however, provide us with a coherent political standpoint; and, although Murimuth was notably hostile both to the papacy and to the English episcopate, there is scarcely any indication in these chronicles (see, for example, the chronicles of Geoffrey le Baker, Robert of Avesbury and the *Annales Paulini*) of support for an identifiable ecclesiastical point of view.[47] The *Vita Edwardi Secundi* is, however, an

---

admittendis, cum in huiusmodi negotiis exequendis sufficienter instructi non fuerint, per aliquem de vestris in talibus edoctum assistentes absentiam nostram excusationis velamine si necesse fuerit dignemini palleare.'

45 *Chronicles of the Reign of Edward I and Edward II*, ed. W. Stubbs (RS, 1882–3), I. lxi–lxvii and Emden, *Oxford*, II. 1329–30.

46 *Adae Murimuth Continuatio Chronicarum*, ed. E. M. Thompson (RS, 1889), p. 30, *Reg. Gravesend*, pp. 207–9, Lunt, *Financial Relations to 1327*, p. 407 and Richardson and Sayles, 'Parliaments of Edward II', p. 84 n. 16.

47 Gransden, *Historical Writing*, II. 25–31, 37–42, 63–71, 77–80.

exception.[48] The unknown author of the *Vita* was plainly a secular clerk, who had respect for learning and a knowledge of both civil and canon law, and whose sympathies were with the lower clergy rather than the prelates. Like Murimuth he was bitterly anti-papal, and he was also opposed to curialist churchmen.[49] He betrays the habits of a preacher: attacking — with frequent references especially to the Old Testament — pride, guile, perjury, greed, material prosperity and 'all the allurements of this life'.[50] One section of his chronicle, at least, presented without any doubt the arguments of the 'communitas cleri': he vigorously defended the lower clergy's opposition to the taxation of their income in 1316, claiming that the king should demand prayers from the bishops and clergy but that the goods of the Church were the goods of the poor.[51]

For the most part the parish clergy, unlike the cathedral chapters, chose as their representatives learned men from among their own midst who were not well-known in royal circles. More often than not they were identified in the proxies by the names of the churches of which they were rectors or vicars, and many of those who were not so identified were probably also beneficed in the dioceses which they represented. A little about a few of them can be gleaned from episcopal registers. Indeed, some of them were involved in episcopal administration. This was true of at least three of the seventeen known proctors of the clergy of the Carlisle diocese: M. John de Boghes and M. Adam de Appelby were successively officials of the bishop of Carlisle and M. William de Goseford acted as the bishop's vicar general in 1311—12.[52] Yet, the parish clergy's proctors figure relatively rarely in the record evidence that has survived. We must beware of assuming that their dedication to local ecclesiastical matters meant that these were men of little ability, or initiative, or, indeed, influence. A majority of the many who were styled master had no doubt studied at Oxford. They are among the eighty per cent or so *alumni* who do not appear in the pages of Emden's biographical register.[53] They do not appear there precisely because, by and large, they did not seek fame and fortune outside the dioceses in which they were beneficed. The little evidence which survives about them is itself a mark of their local importance.

[48] *Ibid.*, 31—7 and *Vita Ed. II*, ed. Denholm-Young, pp. xix—xxviii.
[49] *Ibid.*, pp. 45—7.
[50] *Ibid.*, pp. 63, 70, 74, 92, 100—2.
[51] *Ibid.*, pp. 76—8.
[52] *Reg. Halton*, I. 85, 250, 263, II. 37—9, 102.
[53] T. H. Aston, 'Oxford's medieval alumni', *Past & Present*, 74 (Feb. 1977), 5.

6

Conclusion

Since the appointing of proctors was a common procedure of the time, essential for the prosecution of business of all kinds, it might seem, on the face of it, unlikely that the proctors of the lesser clergy in parliament saw themselves as distinctive.[1] Certainly the same men chosen by cathedral chapters to serve in parliament also acted as proctors on other commissions and in other courts of law. But the letters of proxy bear witness that proctors were given distinct powers for particular business. They were not proctors full stop, but always proctors to do this or that. When the archdeacon of Hereford appointed Walter de Lugwardyn as his proctor for the parliament of Northampton of 1307, the archdeacon described himself as proctor of the dean and chapter of Hereford for the process of canonisation of Thomas Cantilupe.[2] There was a world of difference between one proctorial commission and another.[3] And the particular and especial nature of proctorial powers for parliament is highlighted in respect of the diocesan clergy for they very rarely appointed proctors for any other business than representation in ecclesiastical or royal assemblies.[4]

F. M. Powicke argued, as long ago as 1939, against what we may

[1] See Denton, 'Clergy and parliament', p. 103.
[2] PRO SC10/1/37.
[3] See R. Brentano, *Two Churches: England the Italy in the Thirteenth Century* (Princeton, 1968), pp. 25–48, J. E. Sayers, 'Canterbury proctors of the court of "Audientia Litterarum Contradictarum"', *Traditio*, 22 (1966), 311–45, and 'Proctors representing British interests at the papal court 1198–1415' in *Proceedings of Third International Congress of Medieval Canon Law*, ed. S. Kuttner (Monumenta Iuris Canonici, Series C: Subsidia, vol. 4, 1971), pp. 143–63, P. N. R. Zutschi, 'Proctors acting for English petitioners in the Chancery of the Avignon Popes (1305–1378)', *Journal of Eccles. Hist.*, 35 (1984) 15–29, and above p. 36. n. 74.
[4] Above p. 28.

call a narrow constitutionalism in assessing the early stages in the development of the English parliament. The early history of parliament, he believed, should be studied in relation to the nature of English society. 'We are not looking for needles in a haystack, but at a stack of needles, capable of different degrees of magnetism'.[5] Powicke's comments did not prevent a concentration of effort upon the search for the origins of the lay commons, a focusing upon the knights of the shire either as representatives in parliament or as petitioners in parliament. Nor did Powicke's comments prevent the search for references to parliament in chancery, exchequer and judicial records, as though an understanding of the emergence of parliament was to be found exactly here or exactly there. In this searching too sharp a line has been drawn between parliaments and ecclesiastical councils or convocations, and the political importance of the lower clergy in both institutions has been largely overlooked. Even Maude Clarke, who strongly opposed both these trends, thought in an over-rigid way about the estates of the realm in parliament, largely because the *Modus Tenendi Parliamentum*, schematic by its very nature, was at the centre of her study.[6] As a result, a particular question in relation to the lower clergy was pushed to the fore: when did they cease to be an estate in parliament?[7] But contemporaries did not think in these stark terms.

Nevertheless, attempts to concentrate on elements, however small, from which parliament grew, are not entirely to be disparaged. One constitutional factor in the position of the lower clergy deserves emphasis, for there is no doubt that it was of special significance. Although the clergy, on three occasions between 1314 and 1316 and on three occasions between 1321 and 1324,[8] responded in some measure to royal mandates to attend parliament (through the medium of the archiepiscopal summons), yet it is clear that they never lost sight of a right which was peculiar to them: they were not bound to attend parliament. Despite the wishes of Edward I and Edward II, and no matter how important they may have been in one parliament or another, they were never tied to parliament so closely as the knights of the shire and the burgesses.

Another distinguishing factor deserves to be underlined. The ruridecanal chapters electing clerical representatives were the counterparts of the county courts electing lay representatives,[9] but

5   Powicke, 'Recent work on parliament'.
6   See *Representation*, esp. pp. 7–32, 125–53.
7   Above p. 2 n. 4.
8   Above p. 21.
9   Above p. 34.

each of these parties represented different constituents. The knights represented their communities. But the clergy represented the clergy — not their parishioners. Although it is difficult to demonstrate that, up to the early fourteenth century, it was actually the elected lay representatives who presented petitions from the localities, there is a strong probability that this was often the case. And the taxation on lay movables to which the lay representatives gave their consent was not taxation of a particular class but taxation per head of population, including taxation of the clergy's personal wealth, that is income not associated with their ecclesiastical offices. To clinch this crucial issue: the wages of the clerical proctors were paid by the clergy; but the wages of the lay representatives were paid by 'all those below the parliamentary peerage and above the serfs'.[10] Of course, the spiritual life of the parishioners was the direct concern of the clergy. In defending their income and their rights the clergy were defending the cure of souls, the parochial work which included, in theory if not always in practice, the provision of poor-relief[11] as well as the provision of church services. How far the parishioners endorsed the clergy's belief in the distinct and special importance of spiritual matters, and thus the distinct and special importance of the clergy, will never be easy to assess, but we must certainly be wary of belittling the influence and power of the Church in the localities. The fact, however, remains that there was emerging a channel of communication, of complaints upwards from the localities and of publicity downwards from the Crown, which did not directly involve the clergy at all.[12]

If we turn our attention to the political pressures which could be brought to bear, in parliament and through parliament, on the king and his government especially at times of crisis,[13] further distinctions between the rôles of lay and clerical representatives are apparent. The capacity which the knights of the shire possessed to act against misgovernment, an important aspect of their position as complainants and related to the fact that they themselves were links in the administrative chain of government, did not exist for the rectors and vicars. But this is not to say that the lower clergy had

[10] Cam, 'Community of the shire', p. 246 and above p. 59.
[11] See Moorman, *Church Life*, pp. 138—9 and C. R. Cheney, 'Levies on the English clergy for the poor and for the king, 1203', *EHR*, 96 (1981), 577—84.
[12] See Maddicott, 'Parliament and constituencies'.
[13] See Harriss, 'Formation of parliament', pp. 52—60.

no public rôle to perform. One feature of their public respon-
sibilities was embodied in the *Confirmatio Cartarum* of October
1297: Magna Carta and the Charter of the Forest were to be read
twice a year in all cathedral churches, and sentences of excommunication were to be pronounced twice a year against contra-
venors. In June 1298 a procedure which directly involved the
parish clergy was laid down for the denunciation of offenders,
and the sentences of excommunication were renewed at the king's
order in 1301.[14] Two points should, however, be noted about the
clergy's position as defenders of the Charters. They were particularly concerned to use their powers in order to defend their
own rights and property; and ecclesiastical sanctions were
overlooked in the *Articuli Super Cartas* of 1300, which, baldly
declaring that no penalty had been established for offenders
against the terms of the Charters, provided that the Charters were
to be read four times a year before the people in full county court
and that three men of standing were to be chosen in each county
to supervise the observance of the Charters. Also, in the Ordinances of 1311 there is no mention of publication of the new concessions by the Church or of ecclesiastical denunciations, and
copies were sent into every county to be publicly proclaimed
without the aid of the Church. Thus secular measures were again
thought to be sufficient. Even so, although the Ordinances were
primarily a lay plan of reform, Archbishop Winchelsey did
himself initiate a procedure for the publication of the Ordinances
by the Church, the posting of a copy by each bishop in a prominent place in his cathedral church and the publishing of the text
before the clergy and people once a year. In addition, the Church
undertook to excommunicate all infringers.[15] The lower clergy,
meeting in parliament late in 1311 and in ecclesiastical council
early in 1312, cannot fail to have been involved in these matters
of great public concern. While they certainly did not stand alone
as defenders of the public good and guardians of the peace of the
realm, they were still being given their part to play. They were in
a strong position to influence public opinion, and the king continued to recognise this fact when he ordered preaching, prayers
and processions to take place, parish by parish, for the welfare of

---

[14] Denton, *Winchelsey*, pp. 167, 189—92.
[15] *Ibid.*, pp. 262, 264, *Reg. Gandavo*, I. 412—13, K. Edwards, 'Political
importance of bishops', p. 321, J. C. Davies, *The Baronial Opposition
to Edward II* (Cambridge, 1918), pp. 366—7 and Clarke, *Representation*, p. 160.

the royal family and of the kingdom, notably at times of war.[16]

By the end of Edward II's reign the political significance of the lay representatives of the community of the realm is unmistakable. The first steps had been taken towards the creation of a distinct rôle for the lay representatives at the centre of political affairs. Members of the lower clergy were certainly present in the parliament of January 1327 which saw the deposition of Edward II, staged as an act of the whole community. Some clergy, probably elected representatives among them, took an oath, along with the prelates, secular magnates, knights of the shire and burgesses, to support Queen Isabella and her son.[17] But the deputation sent to Edward II at Kenilworth, which was chosen to represent the whole realm, included knights of the shire and burgesses, but no lower clergy. And a letter from the prior of Canterbury to his archbishop, at a date shortly before the meeting of parliament, is perhaps even more telling. The prior suggested that since a deputation of two bishops had failed to persuade the king to come to parliament, a further deputation should be sent: 'an embassy of two earls, two barons, four citizens and burgesses and four knights of the shire, specially chosen by the community of the whole realm'.[18] It is difficult to escape the conclusion that the prior believed that the whole community could be represented without the lower clergy, though certainly not without the knights and burgesses.

It was at this same parliament early in 1327, after the coronation of Edward III on 1 February, that the prelates and clergy presented a set of grievances, of the traditional kind in defence of their own liberties.[19] Also presented was the first full set of commons' petitions, concerned with a great variety of issues, topical rather than

---

[16] See Wright, *Church and Crown*, pp. 348–60 and A. K. McHardy, 'Liturgy and propaganda in the diocese of Lincoln during the Hundred Years War' in *Studies in Church History*, 18, ed. S. Mews (Oxford, 1982), pp. 215–27.

[17] Below p. 115 n. 47.

[18] B. Wilkinson, 'The deposition of Richard II and the accession of Henry IV', *EHR*, 54 (1939), 226–7 (reprinted in Fryde and Miller (eds.), *Historical Studies of the English Parliament*, I. 340–1) and Clarke, *Representation*, pp. 177–8, 186–90 (this chapter is a fuller version of 'Communities of estates and the deposition of Edward II' in *Hist. Essays in Honour of Tait*, ed. J. G. Edwards et al. (Manchester, 1933), pp. 27–45).

[19] *Rot. Parl. Inediti*, pp. 106–10, and see Jones, '*Gravamina* of the clergy', pp. 225–7.

traditional.[20] Included here was the request for a written record of what was granted by the king and council, so that the knights could carry it back to their shire for proclamation, and — clearly unacceptable to the king and council — so that the sworn oaths of the community could be obtained. Included, too, in the commons' petitions were requests of direct concern to the Church. The commons asked that pleas be sent to the pope to refrain from reservations to bishoprics and ecclesiastical benefices, to allow free elections in the English Church and to canonise Thomas of Lancaster and Robert Winchelsey. They asked that the estate of the Church should be maintained in all points along with Magna Carta, and they complained about the attacks upon the temporalities of bishoprics[21] and the proceedings, by use of the writ *quare impedit*, against bishops who refused to institute clerks who had been presented during vacancies.[22] They also protested about the income of churches going to foreigners who lived outside the realm: as a result the people suffered greatly, for they were unable to share in the alms of the Church. However much the clergy were concerned about the affairs of the realm, they continued to complain to the Crown on their own specific behalf; but the commons included in their petitions matters which were directly related to the work of the Church and of the clergy, and in doing so showed an interest in the welfare of parishioners. The contrast between the two kinds of grievances is striking.

But we must not assume that the lay representatives consciously saw themselves as usurping the position of the clergy. This is illustrated in 1334. Among the commons' petitions in the February of that year was included a request that all the bishops publish sentences of excommunication in every parish church against felons and their maintainers, conspirators, disturbers of the peace and their maintainers, and bringers of false pleas and their maintainers.[23] The result was a royal ordinance of 16 March issued to

---

[20] *Rot. Parl. Inediti*, pp. 116–26, and *Rot. Parl.*, II. 7–11; and see Raynor, '"Commune petition"', p. 556 and Harriss, *King, Parliament and Finance*, pp. 121–2.

[21] Referring, no doubt, to the seizure of the temporalities of Orleton and Burghersh, bishops of Hereford and Lincoln: see K. Edwards, 'Political importance of bishops', pp. 335–7, 340, and Haines, *Adam Orleton*, pp. 49, 156, 203.

[22] See W. E. L. Smith, *Episcopal Appointments and Patronage in the Reign of Edward II* (Chicago, 1938), pp. 86–94 and Denton, *Winchelsey*, pp. 274–7.

[23] *Rot. Parl. Inediti*, p. 234.

every bishop (except Adam Orleton whose translation to Winchester Edward III opposed)[24] giving instructions that the excommunications should take place on each Sunday and on each double feast-day in every cathedral church, collegiate church and parish church.[25] The clergy were still acknowledged as important publicity agents. Even so, the initiative of the commons in these matters is a notable new development. The first clause of the commons' petitions in the parliament of March 1340 was a novel request for the redress of any infringements upon the freedom of the Church by the suit of plaintiffs in parliament.[26] And when a committee was set up in this same parliament to consider the 'conditions et requestes touchaunt le clergie', included in its membership were thirteen knights of the shire and six citizens and burgesses — but no proctors of the lower clergy.[27] The content of the 'conditions et requestes' can be deduced from the fourth Statute resulting from the parliament.[28] The Statute, of 16 April, referred to the petitions of the prelates and clergy and made especially wide concessions, including the following: the freedom of all churchmen from prises; the limitation of the royal right of presentation to benefices, when the temporalities of bishoprics were in the king's hands, to a period of three years after the benefice became vacant; and the protection of the estates of bishoprics and royal monasteries from destruction and waste during vacancies. This was a major charter of ecclesiastical liberties.

The clerical petitions which had thus resulted in concessions from the Crown had been, there is no doubt, drawn up in the ecclesiastical council of 27 January 1340.[29] They were conditions for the grant of a tenth by the clergy, and this council, at which the tax was discussed and the conditions drawn up, had met as a result of decisions taken at the Michaelmas parliament of 1339.[30] It had been

---

[24] Haines, *Adam Orleton*, p. 63.

[25] *Foedera*, II. ii. 880, *Concilia*, II. 562, *Reg. Grandisson*, I. 51—2, Bodl., Ashmole 794, fo. 46 and HWRO, Reg. Montacute, p. 8.

[26] Harriss, *King, Parliament and Finance*, pp. 260, 518.

[27] *Rot. Parl.*, II. 113, as noted also in Clarke, *Representation*, p. 150 n. 2. And see Raynor, '"Commune petition"', pp. 559—60, 566.

[28] *Statutes*, I. 292—4, *Concilia*, II. 655—6, *Reg. Grandisson*, I. 61—3, *Reg. Bransford*, pp. 67—8 and WRO, Reg. Wyvil, I, fo. 50. This Statute escaped the attention of Jones, '*Gravamina* of the clergy'. It is discussed with further references in P. C. Saunders, 'Royal Ecclesiastical Patronage in England 1199—1351' (Oxford D.Phil., 1978), pp. 359—70.

[29] See *Reg. Bransford*, p. 512.

[30] *Rot. Parl.*, II. 106.

determined there not only that the next parliament should meet on 20 January 1340 but also that the convocation of Canterbury be summoned to meet at St Paul's on 27 January and the convocation of York on 3 February. In the event, the last of these dates was changed, in the royal writs, to 9 February.[31] The convocations of Canterbury and York had become essential adjuncts of parliament.[32] They were essential for one reason more than any other: direct taxation of the clergy was as important to the Crown, or almost as important, as taxation of lay movables.

The taxation of clerical income for this period leading up to the French war and the political crisis of 1340–1 has yet to be studied in detail. Such a study will require an examination of the position of the abbeys and priories in relation to both parliament and convocation. With many churches appropriated to them, the monasteries drew a large amount of their income from spiritualities, their income as 'rectors'. So abbots and priors had close associations with the diocesan clergy, as well as being estate-owning prelates. The difference between the number of regular clergy summoned to parliaments and the number summoned to convocations was the major distinction in the clerical composition of the two assemblies. But in all tax-granting assemblies their presence in large numbers was important. For the ecclesiastical council of January 1323 the king himself took the unusual step of ordering abbots to be present.[33] The king's order for provincial summonses for the parliament of 1311 had included abbots and priors; and this attempt to bring into parliament the abbots and priors, as summoned to ecclesiastical councils, was revived for the parliament of September 1334 and was repeated for each parliament for which there was a provincial order up to March 1340.[34] The 1330s were a critical period for the representation of monasteries in parliament. If they had representatives in parliament then their temporalities would be included in lay grants of taxation. Abbots who were absent from parliament claimed, in 1338 and 1340, that the income of their houses should be taxed with clerical subsidies, not with taxes granted in parliament.[35] For the religious, as for the secular clergy,

---

[31] *Dignity of a Peer*, IV. 510.
[32] And see above pp. 22–3.
[33] *Parl. Writs*, II. ii. 281–2, BL, Cotton Vesp. E xxi, fo. 51v, and see Clarke, *Representation*, p. 139.
[34] For references see above p. 19 n.5.
[35] For 1338, see *Calendar of Close Rolls 1337–39*, p. 538, *Reg. Shrewsbury*, pp. 374, 381, *Reg. Bransford*, pp. 280–1 and J. G. Edwards, 'Taxation and consent in the court of Common Pleas, 1338',

1340 was a turning-point. From 1340 onwards the greatly reduced list of 'parliamentary' abbots changed little.

Despite these developments, it seems that there had been no radical changes concerning royal taxation of the clergy since the years 1294—1316.[36] To take the first ten years of Edward III's reign, there were five taxes on lay movables (1327, 1332, 1334 and two in 1336) amounting to a total, working from the assessments, of approximately £170,000.[37] During the same period there were six clerical tenths paid to the king, amounting in all to approximately £110,000. These were: half of a papal tenth for four years, ordered in 1330, and four tenths granted directly to the king, in 1327, 1334 and two in 1336.[38] The money raised from clerical subsidies as compared with lay subsidies was probably lower in these years than for the reign as a whole. Between 1336 and 1360 the clergy granted a tenth to the king in every year except two.[39] About two-thirds of the total clerical income being taxed was the income from parish churches, the income of rectors and vicars. By the 1330s the clergy without exception took their decisions about the granting of taxes in convocations; but, if conditions and petitions were attached to

EHR, 57 (1942), 473—82. For 1340, see Chew, *Ecclesiastical Tenants-in-Chief*, pp. 173—5, Clarke, *Representation*, pp. 22—3 and *Calendar of the MSS of the Dean and Chapter of Wells*, I (HMC, 1907), 245 —6.

[36] For which years see Denton, *Winchelsey*, pp. 55—268, 299—301 and *idem*, 'Reynolds and ecclesiastical politics', pp. 253—70. Taxation for the French war has been discussed with little or no reference to clerical taxes: see, for example, E. B. Fryde, 'Parliament and the French war, 1336—40' in *Essays in Medieval History Presented to B. Wilkinson*, ed. T. A. Sandquist and M. R. Powicke (Toronto, 1969), pp. 250—69.

[37] J. F. Willard, 'The taxes upon movables in the reign of Edward III', *EHR*, 30 (1915), 69—74; and see C. Johnson, 'The collectors of lay taxes' in *The English Government at Work 1327—1336*, II, ed. W. A. Morris and J. R. Strayer (Cambridge, Mass., 1947), p. 226 and *The Lay Subsidy of 1334*, ed. R. E. Glasscock (London, 1975), pp. xiii—xvii.

[38] W. E. Lunt, 'The collectors of clerical subsidies granted to the king by the English clergy' in *The English Government at Work*, II, ed. Morris and Strayer, pp. 75—88. A tenth of the assessed clerical income was about £19,000 (see W. Stubbs, *Constitutional History of England*, II (4th edn, 1896), table facing p. 580), though the king's half of the papal quadrennial tenth apparently raised little more than £35,000 (Lunt, *Financial Relations 1327—1534*, p. 87).

[39] See *ibid.*, p. 88 and J. H. Ramsay, *History of the Revenues of the Kings of England*, II (Oxford, 1925), pp. 294—5.

the grants, then the decisions had still to be presented to the king and council in parliament. Perhaps it was especially because of these close links between convocations and parliament that the king continued after 1340 to 'forewarn', through his bishops, the lower clergy to attend parliament.[40]

Although the relative importance of the lay representatives and the clerical representatives in assemblies summoned by the king is not simple to unravel, striking distinctions between the two have thus emerged by 1340. These distinctions, which are not apparent in the *Modus Tenendi Parliamentum*, give definition to the commons which is coming fully into focus as an estate in parliament between 1327 and 1340. While the plenipotentiary powers of the members of the commons lie at the centre of their status as representatives, it was not these powers to act which in themselves differentiated the commons from other representatives.[41] It was certainly not *plena potestas* which made them distinctive. They were distinctive because they were ordered to attend, through the sheriffs, by enforceable writs, because they represented all the free men in their localities, and also because there were unusually close ties in England between the processes of central and of local government. The lower clergy also had to respond when their archbishops ordered them to attend clerical assemblies, by their nature now often closely linked to parliament. But the clergy were a class apart. As already stressed, whether in convocation or in parliament they represented themselves. Churchmen felt under threat from the politics of lay government, and the representatives of shires and boroughs had become an identifiable element in that government.

Yet, the social and political concerns of laity and clergy were intertwined. The sources tell us most about governmental practices and administrative developments and least about links which cut across the jurisdictional preoccupations of kings and bishops. It is thus easier to highlight procedural and legal divisions than to judge how far the king's assemblies truly reflected the social order of the realm. The non-baronial clergy, the spiritual leaders of the parishes, were certainly not silent. They were organised and trained to speak up. Although in their sermons the clergy often reveal a general rather than a particular concern with matters political,[42] their interest in the affairs of the realm is amply

---

[40] McHardy, 'Representation of clergy', esp. p. 107.
[41] Above pp. 37–9.
[42] See G. R. Owst, *Preaching in Medieval England* (Cambridge, 1926) and *Literature and Pulpit in Medieval England* (Cambridge, 1933).

demonstrated. And occasionally we glimpse a local churchman being openly partisan: the vicar of Wigan exhorted his parishioners in 1322 to support Thomas of Lancaster.[43] If we know more especially about the rights which the clergy claimed for themselves, and petitioned to defend, it is because these had to be set down in writing.

Can we describe the developments in representation from the last years of Edward I's reign to the first years of Edward III's reign as an aspect of 'laicisation'? We have in mind the words of J. R. Strayer: 'Laicization may be defined as the development of a society in which primary allegiance is given to lay government, in which final decisions regarding social objectives are made by lay government, in which the Church is merely a private society with no public powers or duties.'[44] Despite the significant enhancement in the rôle of lay representatives and county courts, there seems little in fact to suggest that the Church had fewer public powers or duties. The ecclesiastical claim was, of course, that all the clergy's powers and duties were, by their very nature, public. This is why the notion of 'laicisation' does not match easily with an evaluation of society in the thirteenth and fourteenth centuries. And as tax-payers, on income granted to the Church for pastoral work, the clergy had been brought into a more direct and more regular relationship with the Crown. Immunities from secular exaction belonged to a former age. These financial commitments could be seen as strengthening the public rôle of the clergy, though this was certainly not the point of view of the clergy themselves. The lesson of the proxies is that the clergy were drawn into public negotiations about royal policies which required financial backing from the whole community. Their identity as an English Church was thereby enhanced. The decline in the payment of papal tenths by the clergy is part of the same story. Indeed, after 1336 no pope succeeded in levying a tax by mandate upon the income of the English clergy and voluntary papal subsidies were few and far between.[45]

Steadily increasing royal control of the Church can hardly be denied, and this is a major element in the case for 'laicisation'. The Church gained, in the long run, few concessions from the repeated presentation of grievances, which were largely concerned with the encroachments of the royal courts. It is difficult to overlook the

---

[43] J. R. Maddicott, 'The county community and the making of public opinion in fourteenth-century England', *TRHS*, 5th ser. 28 (1978), 38.

[44] Strayer, 'Laicization of French and English society', p. 76.

[45] Lunt, *Financial Relations 1327–1534*, pp. 75–168.

fact that, when concessions were made to the Church in April 1340, it was through the mediation of the commons. Maitland's words, in the context of the relations between church courts and royal courts, can be used to sum up broad trends: 'The honours were divided; but the state, as by this time its habit was, took the odd trick.'[46] Some aspects of the development of parliament and of the commons suggest that allegiances may well have been moving more towards lay government; and there is certainly a strong case for arguing that an increasing number of decisions regarding social objectives were being made by lay governments. It is noteworthy, too, that, whereas most of Henry III's justices had been clerks, by 1327 royal clerical justices had almost entirely disappeared.[47] But the story of clerical representation in royal assemblies between 1295 and 1340 was clearly not, on their own terms, one of failure for the clergy. From 1295, under the leadership of Robert Winchelsey, to 1340, under the leadership of John Stratford, the English clergy had fought to defend their separate rights. Their campaign had been weakened at times by *curiales*, who promoted conciliatory policies. The constitutional settlement resulting from the parliament of March 1340, with ecclesiastical complaints redressed in the fourth Statute, marks something of a triumph, however shortlived, for the sacerdotalist point of view. And although we cannot ever know exactly how far the stated views of the *communitas cleri*, as in 1297 and 1314—16, were views commonly held by the clergy who served the parishes, the apparent care which generally attended the procedures of representation lead us to suggest that sacerdotalism — belief in the overriding importance of the cure of souls and in the special and protected status of the clergy — was perhaps at least the prevailing opinion of the diocesan clergy. The high-minded attitude of many churchmen was disparaged, we can be sure, by many of the curialist clergy, who served not only the king but often, too, magnates, bishops and large monasteries.[48] But, despite all the evidence for an 'intricate web of lay and clerical activities in English society',[49] it is a mistake to imagine that it was

---

[46] F. W. Maitland, *Canon Law in the Church of England* (London, 1893), p. 54.

[47] J. R. Maddicott, *Law and Lordship: Royal Justices as Retainers in Thirteenth- and Fourteenth-Century England* (Past and Present Supplement 4, 1978), pp. 17—18.

[48] See Cheney, 'Law and letters in fourteenth-century Durham', p. 85 and Denton, *Winchelsey*, pp. 269—96.

[49] F. M. Powicke, *Thirteenth Century* (2nd edn, 1962), pp. 467—9.

only a few idealistic prelates who were fighting for the principles that are evident in the recurrent sets of clerical complaints.[50] It was an aspect of their sacerdotalism that the lower ranks of the clergy, while being willing to send proctors to parliament by choice, had fought to avoid the obligation of attendance. The provincial writ, already in a weakened form since 1327, never re-appeared after March 1340. The right to meet in separate clerical assemblies to discuss royal taxes and all that they entailed was at last secure. The clergy had won a long constitutional struggle, but in practical terms the Crown had lost very little. Convocation had moved into a very close relationship with parliament and would meet at the king's request. These developments mark, nevertheless, a re-affirmation of the division between the clergy and the laity. The ideal of the *Modus Tenendi Parliamentum*, of clerical and lay communities working together in parliament, was not to be.

---

[50] Cf. *ibid.*, p. 459 and W. R. Jones, 'Relations of the two jurisdictions: conflict and co-operation in England during the thirteenth and four-teenth centuries', *Studies in Medieval and Renaissance History*, 7 (1970), 88.

Appendix 1

A SELECTION OF LETTERS OF PROXY FROM THE PUBLIC RECORD OFFICE

(a)   *Proxy of the clergy of the diocese of Bath and Wells for the parliament of 13 October 1307.*

PRO SC10/1/20. 195mm x 68mm (inc. width of partly torn away tongue and wrapping tie).

Universis pateat per presentes quod nos clerus totius Bathoniensis et Wellensis diocesis ordinamus facimus et constituimus dilectos nobis in Christo magistros Hugonem de Pencryz et Robertum Fayrmay clericos nostros veros et legitimos procuratores coniunctim seu divisim ad faciendum et consentiendum hiis que in quindena sancti Michaelis proximo futura apud Norhamton' in parliamento domini Edwardi dei gratia regis Anglie illustris de communi consilio sui regni domino favente contigerit ordinari super negotiis in mandato dicti domini regis nostri contentis, ratum et firmum perpetuo habituri quicquid iidem procuratores in premissis duxerint nomine nostro ut premittitur faciendum. In cuius rei testimonium sigillum officialitatis domini decani Wellensis ad nostram procurationem presentibus est appensum. Dat' Well' die lune proxima post festum sancti Michaelis anno domini m° ccc^mo septimo. (*Wells, 2 October 1307*)

(b)   *Proxy of the clergy of the archdeaconry of Shropshire, in the diocese of Hereford, for the parliament of 13 October 1307.*

PRO SC10/1/28. 220mm x 120mm (inc. width of torn away tongue).

Universis pateat per presentes quod nos rectores vicarii portionarii ceterique de clero archidiaconatus Solops' Herefordensis diocesis, ad comparendum coram illustrissimo rege domino Edwardo dei gratia rege Anglie apud Norhamton' in quindena post festum sancti Michaelis cum continuatione et prorogatione dierum subsequentium una cum prelatis magnatibus et proceribus dicti regni et ad tractandum consilium auxiliumque impendendum necnon ad consentiendum hiis que pro humatione corporis pie memorie domini Edwardi quondam regis Anglie ac solempnitate sponsalium et coronationis dicti domini Edwardi regis nunc regnantis et aliis articulis statum eiusdem regni tangentibus de communi consilio ad honorem dei provisa fuerint inibi vel etiam ordinata, dilectos nobis in Christo dominum Walterum perpetuum vicarium in ecclesia de Clebur' mortum' et magistrum Johannem de Brunsope rectorem ecclesie de Oldebur' procuratores nostros et quemlibet eorum insolidum constituimus facimus et etiam ordinamus, ratum habituri et gratum quicquid iidem procuratores vel alter eorundem in premissis duxerint seu duxerit faciendum. In cuius rei testimonium sigillum venerabilis viri domini officialis Herefordensis ad nostrum rogatum presentibus procuravimus apponi. Dat' apud Lydebur' die veneris proxima ante festum sancti Dyonisii anno domini m° ccc^mo septimo. (*Ledbury, 6 October 1307*)

(c) *Proxy of the clergy of the archdeaconry of Salop, in the diocese of Coventry and Lichfield, for the parliament of 27 April 1309.*

PRO C270/35/17. 210mm x 55mm (tongue cut completely away).
The date of this proxy shows that it was for parliament rather than for an ecclesiastical council (the next council was held in November 1309), and the fact that the clergy of the archdeaconry of Stafford appointed the same two proctors for the parliament of April 1309 (SC10/2/61) indicates that the archdeaconry in question is Salop in the diocese of Coventry and Lichfield rather than Shropshire in the diocese of Hereford.

Universis pateat presentes quod nos communitas beneficiatorum et clerus archidiaconatus Salop' dilectos nobis in Christo magistros magistrum Galfridum de Blasten' canonicum Lichf' et   [1] . .

1 Gap left for name. The rector of Wolfhampcote is named as Robert in SC10/2/61.

rectorem ecclesie de Walfhamcote procuratores nostros veros et legitimos ordinamus facimus et constituimus ad consentiendum nomine nostro hiis que in convocatione sanctorum patrum domini Roberti dei gratia Cantuariensis archiepiscopi totius Anglie primatis et suffraganeorum suorum de statu ecclesie et regni Anglie domino favente coram ipsis fuerint ordinata et ad prestandum in animas nostras quodlibet genus liciti sacramenti et ad omnia alia nomine nostro facienda que circa premissa occurrerint oportuna, ratum habituri et gratum quicquid G. et [2] antedicti faciendum duxerint seu procurandum in premissis. Pro eisdem etiam rem ratam habituri et indicatum solvi exponimus cautiones. In cuius rei testimonium has literas nostras sigillo domini archidiaconi nostri Salop' signatas eisdem G. et [2] fecimus patentes. Dat' Salop' die iovis proxima post dominicam qua cantatur misericordia domini anno domini m° ccc° nono. (*Shrewsbury, 17 April 1309*)

(d) *Proxy of the subprior and chapter of Rochester for the parliament of 18 March 1313.*

PRO SC10/2/100. 210mm x 98mm (inc. width of tongue and torn away wrapping tie).

Universis pateat per presentes quod nos frater Edmundus supprior ecclesie beati Andree apostoli Roff' et eiusdem loci conventus, ad comparendum tertia dominica instantis quadragesime in parliamento excellentissimi principis regis nostri Anglie apud Westmonasterium celebrando, dilectos nobis in Christo fratrem Hamonem de Hethe monachum et magistrum Willelmum de Fakenham clericum coniunctim et divisim et alterum eorum insolidum ita quod non sit melior conditio occupantis procuratores nostros facimus ordinamus et constituimus per presentes, dantes eisdem et eorum alteri potestatem generalem et mandatum speciale una cum aliis procuratoribus religiosorum Anglie nomine nostro ordinandi ac consentiendi hiis que in parliamento antedicto per . . episcopos ac alios prelatos et religiosos ad utilitatem regni domino favente statui contigerit et ordinari necnon alium procuratorem seu alios procuratores loco sui et eorum alterius substituendi ac omnia et singula in premissis et circa premissa faciendi que per veros et legitimos procuratores vel eis substitutos seu substitutum de iure fieri debeant. Pro eisdem vero procuratoribus nostris substituto seu substitutis ab eisdem seu ab eorum altero rem ratam haberi et

2   Gap left for initial.

iudicatum solvi sub ypoteca rerum nostrarum promittimus et exponimus cautiones. In cuius rei testimonium sigillum nostrum ad causas deputatum presentibus duximus apponendum. Dat' Roff' ii nonas Martii anno domini m° ccc^mo duodecimo. (*Rochester, 6 March 1313*)

(e)   *Proxy of the archdeacon of Carlisle and clergy of the diocese of Carlisle for the parliament of 20 January 1315.*

PRO SC10/4/157. 220mm x 78mm (inc. width of tongue torn away). The right-hand side of the document is damaged, and suggested readings for missing words are supplied within square brackets.

Universis pateat per presentes quod nos . . archidiaconus et clerus civitatis et diocesis Karleolensis de unanimi consensu omnium de clero dil[ectos nobis] in Christo dominum Hugonem de Burgo rectorem ecclesie de Burgo sub Mora et dominum Robertum de Appelby rectorem [   ]³ Karleolensis diocesis procuratores nostros coniunctim et divisim ad comparendum pro nobis et nostro nomine in instanti parliamento [domini regis apud] Westmonasterium in octabis sancti Hillarii ordinamus facimus et constituimus per presentes, dantes eisdem et eorum alteri plenam [et liberam potestatem] ac speciale mandatum ad tractandum faciendum et consentiendum omnibus et singulis que tunc de communi consilio super negotiis st[atum regni tangentibus] in prefato parliamento favente domino contigerit ordinari, ratum et gratum habituri quicquid iidem procuratores vel eorum [alter] faciendum duxerint in premissis. In cuius rei testimonium sigillum venerabilis patris domini Johannis dei gratia Karleolensis episcopi presentibus [apponi] procuravimus. Dat' apud Meleburn' xviii kalendas Februarii anno domini m° ccc^mo quartodecimo. (*Melbourne, Derbyshire, 15 January 1315*)

---

3   A Robert de Appelby became rector of Brougham (Cumbria) in June 1310, and perhaps the same Robert de Appelby became rector of Bolton (Cumbria) in Jan. 1311: *Reg. Halton*, II. 17–18, 24.

(f) *Proxy of the clergy of the York diocese for the parliament of 20 October 1318.*

PRO SC10/6/255. 250mm x 80mm (inc. width of tongue and torn away wrapping tie).

Universis pateat per presentes quod nos clerus Eboracensis diocesis de unanimi consensu omnium de clero dilectos nobis in Christo magistros Johannem de Skyrne rectorem ecclesie de Marton' in Craven et Johannem de Lutton' rectorem medietatis ecclesie de Rillington' dicte diocesis procuratores nostros ad comparendum pro nobis et nostro nomine in instanti parliamento domini regis apud Ebor' a die sancti Michaelis ultimo preterito in tres septimanas ordinamus facimus et constituimus per presentes, dantes eisdem plenam et liberam potestatem ac speciale mandatum ad tractandum faciendum et consentiendum omnibus et singulis que tunc de communi consilio super negotiis statum regni tangentibus in prefato parliamento favente domino contigerit ordinari, ratum et gratum habituri quicquid iidem procuratores nostro nomine faciendum duxerint in premissis. In cuius rei testimonium sigillum officialitatis curie Ebor' procuravimus hiis appendi. Dat' Ebor' xv kalendas Novembris anno domini millesimo trecentesimo decimo octavo. (*York, 18 October 1318*)

(g) *Proxy of the prior and chapter of Ely for the parliament of 15 July 1321.*

PRO SC10/7/325. 235mm x 100mm (inc. width of torn away tongue and wrapping tie).

Pateat universis per presentes quod nos frater Johannes prior Elien' et eiusdem loci capitulum, ad comparendum pro nobis et nomine nostro in instanti parliamento excellentissimi principis ac domini nostri karissimi domini Edwardi dei gratia illustris regis Anglie domini Hibernie et ducis Aquitannie apud Westmonasterium a die nativitatis sancti Johannis baptiste proximo futura in tres septimanas super diversis et arduis negotiis eundem regem et dominum nostrum et statum regni sui specialiter tangentibus dante domino tenendo et celebrando, necnon ad tractandum et consulendum in eodem parliamento cum prelatis magnatibus et proceribus dicti regni, ac etiam ad faciendum et pleno consentiendum omnibus et singulis que tunc ibidem de communi consilio favente domino ordinari contigerit super negotiis antedictis, dilectos nobis in Christo fratrem Johannem de Conigton' commonachum nostrum et magistrum Henricum de Thrippelowe clericum coniunctim et divisim et quemlibet eorum insolidum ita quod non sit melior conditio occupantis sed quod unus eorum inceperit alter libere poterit adimplere procuratores nostros veros et legittimos ordinamus facimus et constituimus per presentes, ratum habituri et gratum quicquid dicti procuratores nostri seu eorum alter de communi consilio prelatorum magnatum et procerum regni supradicti duxerint seu duxerit faciendum in premissis. In cuius rei testimonium sigillum commune capituli nostri presentibus fecimus apponi. Dat' apud Ely in capitulo nostro vi die mensis Julii anno domini m° ccc^{mo} vicesimo primo et regni ipsius regis et domini nostri quartodecimo. (*Ely, 6 July 1321*).

(h) *Proxy of the clergy of the archdeaconry of Durham for the parliament of 26 November 1330.* (See Appendix 3)

PRO SC10/14/694. 230mm x 85mm (inc. width of torn away tongue). Endorsed: Dunolm'.

Pateat universis per presentes quod nos clerus archidiaconatus Dunolmensis dilectum nobis in Christo magistrum Johannem de Bekyngham clericum per presentes literas nostrum facimus et constituimus procuratorem, ad comparendum et interessendum pro nobis et nomine nostro in parliamento domini nostri domini Edwardi dei gratia regis Anglie illustris apud Westmonasterium die lune proxima post festum sancte Katerine virginis proximo futurum, necnon ad faciendum et consentiendum hiis que tunc ibidem de communi consilio divina favente clementia ordinari contigerit super negotiis in eodem parliamento expediendis, et ad substituendum alium procuratorem loco sui si sibi viderit expedire, et ad omnia alia facienda in premissis et ea contingentibus que necessaria fuerint vel oportuna etiam si mandatum speciale requirant, pro dicto vero procuratore nostro et substituendo ab eodem rem ratam haberi et iudicatum solvi sub ypotheca rerum nostrarum promittimus et exponimus cautiones. In cuius rei testimonium sigillum officii domini Dunolmensis . . episcopi . . vicarii generalis presentibus est appensum. Dat' Dunolm' xiiii die Novembris anno domini millesimo trecentesimo tricesimo. (*Durham, 14 November 1330*)

(i) *Proxy of the chapter of Worcester for the parliament of 19 September 1334.*

PRO C219/5/17/25. 255mm x 60mm (tongue cut completely away). The left-hand side of the document is damaged, and suggested readings for missing words are given in square brackets.

Excellentissimo principi et domino domino Edwardo dei gratia regi Anglie illustri capitulum ecclesie cathedralis Wygorniensis subiectionem omnimodam cum omni reverentia et honore [debitis] regie maiestati. Noverit excellentia vestra quod nos dilectum nobis in Christo dominum Thomam de Evesham clericum nostrum procuratorem verum et legitimum [facimus] ordinamus et constituimus per presentes ad faciendum omnia et singula que in parliamento vestro die lune proxima post festum exaltationis sancte Crucis [apud] Westmonasterium celebrando cum continuatione et prorogatione dierum tunc sequentium iuxta formam vim et effectum premunitionis facte nobis in hac parte per [dominum] venerabilem patrem dominum Simonem dei gratia Wygorniensem episcopum facere deberemus, dantes eidem substituendi potestatem ad premissa procuratorem alium loco sui [substitutum]que revocandi et procuratoris officium reassumendi quotiens et quando viderit oportunum, ratum habituri et gratum quicquid per eundem Thomam seu substi[tutum ab] eo nomine nostro factum fuerit in premissis. In cuius rei testimonium sigillum nostrum commune fecimus hiis apponi. Dat' in capitulo nostro Wygorn' vii idus [Septem]bris anno domini millesimo trecentesimo tricesimo quarto. (*Worcester, 7 September 1334*)

(j) *Proxy of the chapter of Durham for the parliament of 26 May 1335.*

PRO SC10/19/929. 250mm x 82mm (inc. width of partly torn away tongue and wrapping tie).

Tenore presentium pateat universis quod nos . . capitulum ecclesie Dunolmensis dilectum nobis in Christo magistrum Robertum de Neunham clericum nostrum procuratorem attornatum et nuntium facimus specialem, ad comparendum et interessendum pro nobis et nomine nostro coram serenissimo principe et domino nostro domino Edwardo dei gratia rege Anglie illustri in instanti parliamento suo apud Ebor' in crastino Ascensionis dominice favente altissimo celebrando, et ad tractandum cum eodem domino nostro ac ceteris regni sui proceribus et prelatis super statum dicti regni contingentibus et aliis omnibus super quibus ibidem tractari contigerit, necnon ad conscentiendum hiis que in predicto parliamento suo de communi consilio procerum et prelatorum regni sui pro utilitate eiusdem salubriter contigerint ordinari, ratum et firmum habituri quicquid prefatus procurator noster nomine nostro fecerit in premissis. In cuius rei testimonium sigillum commune capituli nostri presentibus duximus apponendum. Dat' Dunolm' in capitulo nostro xx^{mo} die Maii anno domini millesimo ccc^{mo} xxx^{mo} quinto. (*Durham, 20 May 1335*)

(k) *Proxy of the clergy of the archdeaconry of Durham for the parliament of 26 May 1335.*

PRO SC10/19/944. 230mm x 125mm (inc. width of tongue and torn away wrapping tie).

Universis pateat per presentes quod nos clerus archidiaconatus Dunolmensis dilectum nobis in Christo magistrum Willelmum de Alverton' perpetuum vicarium de Acley Dunolmensis diocesis procuratorem nostrum et nuntium specialem ordinamus facimus et constituimus per presentes, dantes et concedentes eidem potestatem generalem et mandatum speciale ad comparendum et interessendum pro nobis et nomine nostro in parliamento serenissimi principis et domini nostri domini Edwardi dei gratia regis Anglie illustris apud Ebor' die veneris in crastino Assencionis domini proximo futura cum continuatione et prorogatione dierum subsequentium, et ad tractandum cum ceteris de clero ibidem existentibus super quibuscumque negotiis dictum dominum nostrum regem et regnum contingentibus prout et quatenus ad nos attinet, et ad consentiendum hiis que in dicto parliamento de consilio regni salubriter ordinari contigerint, et ad dissentiendum ubicumque quotienscumque et quandocumque opus fuerit et sibi videbitur pro nobis expedire, necnon quascumque excusationes legitimas nobis competentes pro nobis et nomine nostro allegandum et proponendum et super eisdem si necesse fuerit iurandum, et plenam fidem que requiritur super hiis faciendum aliaque omnia et singula faciendum et exercendum que in premissis et circa premissa necessaria fuerint congrua seu oportuna etiam si mandatum exigant speciale, ratum gratum et firmum habituri quicquid idem magister

Willelmus procurator predictus in premissis et circa premissa duxerit faciendum. In cuius rei testimonium sigillum officialitatis
Dunolmensis presentibus apponi procuravimus. Dat' Dunolm' xvi
kalendas Junii domini m° ccc^mo tricesimo quinto. (*Durham, 17 May
1335*)

(l)   *Proxy of the clergy of the diocese of York for the parliament
      of 29 March 1340.*

      PRO SC10/22/1098. 130mm x 97mm (inc. width of partly
      torn away tongue and wrapping tie).

Excellentissimo principi et domino domino Edwardo dei gratia regi
Anglie et Francie et domino Hibernie . . clerus diocesis Eboracensis
quicquid poterit reverentie grex pusillus. Licet virtute premunitionis vel assignationis cuiuscumque excepta dumtaxat auctoritate
domini nostri pape de iure non teneamur qualitercumque extra
Ebor' provinciam comparere, ob reverentiam tamen regie
maiestatis et presentie vestre corporalis quas offendere for-
midamus, dilectos nobis in Christo magistros Robertum de
Neuwenham et Johannem de Aslakby clericos procuratores
nostros, ad comparendum coram vobis in parliamento apud
Westmonasterium die mercurii proximo post diem dominicam in
medio quadragesime proximo futuram tenendo, ac ad allegandum
et ostendendum causas absentie nostre et ipsam absentiam nostram
effectualiter excusandum, necnon ad faciendum et recipiendum
ulterius quod ad excusatoris officium pertinere dinoscitur, constituimus per presentes, ratum et gratum habituri quicquid iidem
procuratores nostro nomine in hac parte duxerint faciendum. In
cuius rei testimonium sigillum officialitatis curie Ebor' procuravimus hiis apponi. Dat' Ebor' xv kalendas Aprilis anno domini
millesimo ccc^mo tricesimo nono. (*York, 18 March 1340*)

Appendix 2

Copy in a Lincoln Chapter Act Book of the certificate of execution of the bishop's summons and of three alternative proxies of the chapter for the parliament of 18 November 1325. (See above pp. 68–9)

LAO, Lincoln Dean and Chapter Archives, A/2/23, fo. 5. The certificate and the proxies follow a copy of Bishop Burghersh's summons, dated 25 October 1325, incorporating the royal writ to the bishop dated 10 October. William Wake's edition of the proxies (*State of the Church,* app. pp. 53–4) is highly abbreviated and inaccurate.

Certificatio capituli reverendo in Christo patri etc. Nos igitur in premissis facere deo dante proponimus quod premunitio vestra predicta exigit et requirit, quod paternitati vestre innotescimus per presentes. Reverendam vestram conservet altissimus ad ecclesie vestre regimen et honorem. Dat' Linc' viii idus Novembris anno supradicto. (*Lincoln, 6 November 1325*) Quarum litterarum auctoritate dictum capitulum constituit duos procuratores videlicet magistros Johannem de Hagh rectorem ecclesie de Langton' et Johannem de Notingham coniunctim et divisim ordinando sibi tria procuratoria, quorum unum fuit plus ceteris restrictum, et si oportuerit utendum,[4] secundum aliquantulum restrictum, et utendum si de alio non possit evadi, tertium magis generale et nullo modo utendum nisi in causa valde necessaria. Tenor vero primi procuratorii restricti talis est: Universis ad quos presentes littere pervenerint pateat per easdem quod nos capitulum ecclesie Lincolniensis cathedralis ordinavimus fecimus et constituimus dilectos nobis in Christo magistros Johannem de Hagh rectorem ecclesie de Langton' Lincolniensis diocesis et Johannem de Notingham

4   et si oportuerit utendum *added in margin with inclusion sign.*

clericum presentium exhibitores nostros veros et legitimos procuratores coniunctim et divisim et quemlibet eorum insolidum ad
comparendum pro nobis in parliamento serenissimi principis et
domini nostri domini Edwardi dei gratia regis Anglie illustris apud
Westmonasterium in octabis sancti Martini proximo futuris tenendo ad tractandum cum prelatis magnatibus et proceribus regni
Anglie super quibusdam magnis et arduis negotiis statum regni
predicti tangentibus necnon ad consentiendum nostro nomine de
consilio et consensu prelatorum et cleri in dicto parliamento con-
gregandorum hiis que ad honorem dicte ecclesie sue sancte ac
utilitatem regni predicti divina disponente clementia ibidem contigerit salubriter ordinari (*fo. 5v*) quatenus ad ista facienda de iure
artari poterimus et debemus, proviso quod iidem procuratores vel
eorum alter nulli contributioni faciende nobis consentiant vel consentiat inconsultis, ratum gratum et firmum habentes quicquid dicti
procuratores nostri vel eorum alter in eventu predicto ad honorem
dei et ecclesie Anglicane atque regni et rei pupplice utilitatem de
consilio et consensu dictorum prelatorum et cleri in hiis ad que de
iure tenentur ut pretangitur fecerint seu fecerit in hac parte. In cuius
rei testimonium has litteras nostras scribi fecimus patentes sigilli
nostri appensione munitas. Dat' in capitulo nostro Linc' vi idus
Novembris anno domini millesimo ccc^mo vicesimo quinto. (*Lincoln,
8 November 1325*) Tenor vero secundi procuratorii aliquantulum
restricti si per primum non possit evadi talis est: 'Pateat etc.' usque
ibi 'proviso' talis hinc[5] incipiendo 'ratum et gratum etc.' usque in
finem. Tenor vero tertii procuratorii generalis et nullo modo ex-
ercendi nisi in causa valde necessaria talis est: 'Pateat universis etc.'
usque ibi 'quatenus ad ista etc.' et incipiendo 'ratum gratum etc.' usque in finem.

---

5   talis hinc *interlined*.

Appendix 3

Acquittance by Hugh de Corbrig' collector of expenses of the proctor of the clergy of the archdeaconry of Durham for the parliament of 26 November 1330. (See above p. 57)

Durham, Dean and Chapter Muniments, Locellus xix no. 90. 215mm x 65 mm.
Hugh de Corbrig' was collector in the archdeaconry of Durham of the expenses of the proctor Master John de Bechingham (for his proxy see PRO SC10/14/694, Appendix 1(h)), and the acquittance is in respect of 6s-7d from the benefices of Master John de Insula, dean of Auckland.

Pateat universis per presentes quod ego Hugo de Corbrig', perpetuus vicarius ecclesie de Pittington, decanus Dunelmensis, collector singulorum denariorum de singulis libris beneficiorum ecclesiasticorum archidiaconatus Dunelmensis per clerum dicti archidiaconatus concessorum pro expensis magistri Johannis de Bechingham versus parliamentum apud London' ultimo celebratum transeuntis pro nova taxatione querenda deputatus, recepi de reverendo viro magistro Johanne de Insula decano ecclesie de Auckland pro beneficiis suis[6] quinque solidos et xix denarios[7] argenti, de quibus fateor me esse perpacatum. Dictum magistrum Johannem acquieto per presentes. In cuius rei testimonium presentibus sigillum apposui. Dat' Dunelm' die mercurii proximo ante festum Epiphanie anno domini m° ccc^mo tricesimo. (*Durham, 2 January 1331*)

6 For the benefices of John de Insula see Emden, *Oxford*, III. 2185 (correcting *Fasti Dunelmenses*, ed. D. S. Boutflower (Surtees Soc., 139, 1926), I. 67). John probably still held the church of Boldon and a portion in the church of Darlington as well as the deanship of Auckland, at a combined assessment of £52-6s-8d (*Taxatio*, pp. 329–30 and *Reg. Kellawe*, III. 98, 102–3); but his payment of 6s-7d, on a levy of 1d in the pound, meant that the total value of his benefices in the archdeaconry of Durham was £79.
7 Illegible word interlined.

Appendix 4

Copy in a Durham register of a letter from the prior of Durham, William de Couton, probably dated 25 May 1335 and probably sent to the proctor Robert de Neunham. (See above p. 36 n. 72 and p. 52)

BL, Cotton Faustina A vi, fo. 17r.

This letter, dated simply Ascension Day, is found among a section of the register which contains letters from the early part of Edward III's reign. It refers to a summons having been received to a parliament to be held. It could possibly refer to the Westminster parliament summoned on 15 May for 15 July 1321. Ascension Day in 1321 was 28 May. But it is much more likely that it refers to the York parliament summoned on 1 April for 26 May 1335. Ascension Day in 1335 was 25 May. The letter was concerned with two proxies which had been drawn up on behalf of the prior and of the chapter, and it was apparently sent to a proctor named in these proxies. The single proctor named in the extant proxy of the chapter of Durham, and also in the separate extant proxy of the prior of Durham, for the parliament of 26 May 1335 (both proxies were dated 20 May) was 'magister Robertus de Neunham clericus noster': PRO SC10/19/929 (see Appendix 1(j)) and /931.

Dilecto etc. De vestra circumspectione plurimum confidentes, duo procuratoria vobis intimamus ad comparendum pro nobis in parliamento futuro, si necesse fuerit, et etiam pro conventu, iuxta formam citationis ad idem parliamentum nobis facte. Unde dilectionem vestram requirimus et rogamus quatinus offerente se necessitate et non aliter dicta procuratoria domino Michaeli de Wath,[8] qui ad huiusmodi procuratoria recipienda se solebat

8 Michael de Wath was keeper of the rolls of Chancery from 1334 to 1337. From

intromittere, liberetis. Ab experimento tam didicimus temporibus retroactis quod non est necesse talia procuratoria per (sic) nobis ostendere nec in parliamento quomodolibet comparere, sed si audieritis nova aliqua in hac parte subito exoriri operemini iuxta ea. Valete. Dat' Dunelm' die Ascenc'.

Dec. 1339 to Feb. 1340 he was one of the keepers of the king's seal, and in 1340 one of the receivers of petitions in parliament. See T. F. Tout, *Chapters in the Administrative History of Medieval England* (Manchester, 1920—33), III. 5, 43, 103, VI. 13, *Rot. Parl.*, II. 112, *Rot. Parl. Inediti*, p. 232, and B. Wilkinson, *The Chancery Under Edward III* (Manchester, 1929), esp. pp. 157—8.

Appendix 5

LIST OF PROCTORS OF DIOCESAN CLERGY AND CATHEDRAL CHAPTERS IN PARLIAMENT FROM NOVEMBER 1295 TO MARCH 1340.

Except where there is a footnote to the contrary each item in this list refers to a letter of proxy. Some proxies from priors of cathedral chapters (enregistered along with the letters from the cathedral chapter) are also referred to in the footnotes, but many more are extant than are noted here, especially among the ecclesiastical proxies under the classification SC10 in the Public Record Office. For the writs of summons, to which the proxies were a response, see the references in Powicke and Fryde (eds.), *Handbook of British Chronology* and above pp. 18 – 23. Every parliament to which the lower clergy were summoned, and which actually met, between November 1295 and March 1340 is included in the list. Round brackets are used for editorial additions. Square brackets indicate information which cannot be supplied by the source in question, usually because of illegibility or damage to the document; where another document can supply the missing information, this is added within the square brackets.

Parliament	Diocese/archdeaconry or cathedral chapter	Names of proctors	Source
1295 (13 Nov. prorogued to) 27 Nov.[9] Westminster	Prior and chapter of Canterbury Prior and chapter of Bath (for 13 Nov.)/subprior and chapter (for 27 Nov.)	G. de Chileham and R. de Clyve, monks William de Hampton, monk	*Parl. Writs*, I. ii. 34 (from CUL, Ee.v.31, fo. 66v) *Parl. Writs*, I. ii. 31, 34 (from LI, Hale 185, fo. 102v)
1296 3 Nov.[9] Bury St Edmunds	Prior and chapter of Canterbury Prior and chapter of Durham	J. de Hardres and J. de Thaneto, monks [ ]	*Parl. Writs*, I. ii. 49 (from CUL, Ee.v.31, fo. 68v) Durham, Cathedral Library, C.IV.24, fo.105v[10]
1300 6 March[11] London	Prior and chapter of Bath	William de Hampton, monk	*Brief Reg.*, ed. Prynne, I. 119 (from LI, Hale 185, fo. 81r)[12]

---

[9]   Expenses paid to proctors of clergy of Ely diocese for this parliament: Lowry, 'Clerical proctors', p. 448.
[10] Among the collection here of miscellaneous letters etc. of c. 1300 there are two undated proxies for a parliament at Bury St Edmunds, one addressed to the king from the prior of Durham and the other openly addressed from the prior and convent. Both proxies appoint one monk, but with gemmipunctus in place of his name.
[11] The king's writ was executed in the diocese of Lincoln by Nicholas de Whitchurch, official of Lincoln *sede vacante* (see *Reg. Winchelsey*, pp. 369 – 70). The subdean and chapter of Lincoln wrote to Nicholas (on 22 Feb. 1300) promising to send a proctor to the parliament to act in their name 'iuxta consilium et assensum cleri Cantuariensis provincie qui tunc ibidem fuerit': LAO, Lincoln D. & C. Archives, Dii/59/1 no. 4. Nicholas ordered a proctor to be sent from each archdeaconry to a meeting at Northampton on 2 March at which the proctors for the whole diocese would be chosen; the official of the archdeacon of Bedford notified him that the clergy of the archdeaconry of Bedford had chosen John de Clare to be sent to this meeting, and likewise the official of the archdeacon of Northampton that the clergy of the archdeaconry of Northampton had chosen Henry de Stoke, rector of Ravensthorpe (Dii/59/1 nos. 3, 5). Concerning the sending of proctors from the Worcester diocese see Clarke, *Representation*, pp. 129 – 30 and above p. 50.
[12] Separate proxy from prior of Bath, also appointing William de Hampton.

Parliament	Diocese/archdeaconry or cathedral chapter	Names of proctors	Source
1305 28 Feb.[13] Westminster	Prior and chapter of Canterbury Chapter of Worcester	John de Thaneto, precentor N. and O. monks	Parl. Writs, I. ii. 140 (from CUL, Ee.v.31, fo. 102r) Worcester, D. & C. Muniments, Liber Albus, fo. 23r (printed Wake, State of the Church, app. p. 31 and calendared Liber Albus, ed. Wilson, p. 18)[14]
	Clergy of Lincoln diocese	M. Henry de Stok', rector of Ravensthorpe (Northants.) and M. John de Fletburg', rector of Hougham (Lincs.)	Wake, State of the Church, app. p. 31 (from LAO, Reg. III (Dalderby), fo. 79)
1307 20 Jan Carlisle	Dean and chapter of Wells	M. Thomas de Luggore and William de Cherleton, canons	Parl. Writs, I. ii. 185—6 (from PRO, C153/1, fos. 130v—132r)[15]
	Chapter of Worcester	John de Sancto Brevello, monk, and William de Thorntoft	
	Subprior and chapter of Rochester	Robert, rector of Hoo (Kent)	
	Chapter of Lincoln	M. Robert de Pykering and Hugh de Normanton', canons	
	Chapter of Exeter	Henry de Pynkeneie, rector of Honiton (Devon)	
	Chapter of Chichester	M. Clement de Peccham, canon	
	Chapter of Salisbury	M. John de Tarenta and M. William de Buckstanes	
	Dean and chapter of York	Adam de Osgodby, canon	
	Prior and chapter of Winchester	Ralph de Canne, monk, and John de Burn'	
	Chapter of Ely	M. Richard de Dene	
	Chapter of Norwich	M. Hugh de Swafham, Thomas de Fuldon' and William de Tutington'	
	Chapter of Hereford	Walter de Lugwardyn and John Craft	
	Chapter of St Asaph	Madoc Goch, canon, and Howell, rector of Llanarmon (Clwyd)	
	Viceregent of the dean and the chapter of St Paul's London	M. John de Bedeford	
	Chapter of Rochester	Robert de Brok'	
	Subprior and chapter of Durham	Hugh de Monte Alto and Thomas de Killington, monks[16]	

[13] Expenses paid to proctors of clergy of Ely diocese for this parliament: Page, Estates of Crowland, p. 63.

[14] Also, proxy of the prior naming Gilbert de Madel' and N. Norton, monks, ('A. & B.' in Wake's edition) and proxy of the prior as proctor of the archdeacon of Worcester (Francis Neapoleonis, cardinal deacon) naming J. de Bremesgrave, monk ('R.B.' in Wake's edition, which also should read 'prior . . . procurator, actor et negotiorum gestor').

[15] All the items for this parliament are from a list of ecclesiastical proctors which was presumably compiled by a clerk of the parliament who had the original letters of proxy, 114 in all, before him. The list survives in the Vetus Codex (PRO, C153/1) and is a copy of a roll only one membrane of which survives (PRO, SC9/15). It was printed in Rot. Parl., I. 189—91, apparently from the earlier edition in W. Ryley, Placita Parliamentaria (1661), pp. 321—6, and duplicating Ryley's errors. Palgrave, however, in Parl. Writs, I. ii. 184—6, provided an accurate transcript. For discussion of the list see above esp. pp. 44—8.

[16] A proxy of the subprior, vicar general of the absent prior, and chapter of Durham was copied on to the dorse of a mandate of the archbishop of York dated 2 July 1306 concerning the appointment to the vicarage of Heighington: Durham, D. & C. Muniments, Misc. Ch. 6190. This undated proxy, for the parliament 'at Carlisle or at Lanercost or wherever it may be held', named, in addition to Hugh de Monte Alto and Thomas de Killington, a third monk, Thomas de Bannburg. 'Thomam de Killington' is interlined and 'Johannem de Castro Bernard' is deleted.

Parliament	Diocese/archdeaconry or cathedral chapter	Names of proctors	Source
1307 20 Jan. Carlisle (contd.)	Clergy of Lincoln diocese	M. Peter de Medeburn, rector of Ingoldsby (Lincs.), professor of canon law, and M. John de Horkestow', rector of Harrington (Lincs.)	(Also, see the proxy in LAO, Reg. III (Dalderby), fos. 108v – 109r)
	Clergy of Worcester archdeaconry	Reginald le Porter, rector of Bourton-on-the-Water (Gloucs.)	
	Clergy of Exeter diocese	M. Thomas Crabbe and M. Ralph de Stok'	
	Clergy of Bath and Wells diocese	M. Hugh de Walmesford and M. Henry de Moneketon	
	Clergy of Rochester diocese	Robert, rector of Hoo (Kent), and Peter, vicar of Yalding (Kent)	
	Clergy of Chichester archdeaconry	Nicholas de Dynneslee, vicar of Bosham	
	Clergy of Ely diocese	M. Richard de Conygton' and M. Adam Eliott	
	Clergy of Durham diocese	M. Adam de Morpath' and John de Pampesworth'	
	Clergy of York diocese	M. John Frаunceis, rector of Wheldrake (N. Yorks.), and William de Bergh, rector of Thornton Dale (N. Yorks.)	
	Clergy of Salisbury diocese	M. William de Buckestanes and M. John de Trenta	
	Clergy of Surrey archdeaconry[17]	M. Richard de Barton' and M. Hugh de Tychewell (Hugh appointed John de Brantingham as his substitute)	
	Clergy of Winchester archdeaconry[17]	M. Richard Wodeloc and M. Hugh de Tychewell[18]	
	Clergy of London diocese	M. William de Melford' and Roger de Arewold', chaplain	
	Clergy of Lewes archdeaconry	M. William de Malmesbury	
	Clergy of Suffolk and Sudbury archdeaconries	M. John Hardy, rector of Thurlow (Suff.)	
	Clergy of Norwich and Norfolk archdeaconries	M. Hugh de Swafham	
	Clergy of Shropshire archdeaconry	William, rector of Silvington (Salop), and Walter de Lugwardyn, rector of Munsley (Heref. & Worc.)	
	Clergy of Carlisle diocese	M. John de Boghes, M. William de Goseford, Robert de Suthayk' and Adam de Appelby	
	Clergy of St Asaph diocese	Madoc Goch, canon, and Howel, rector of Llanarmon (Clwyd)	
	Clergy of Gloucester archdeaconry	M. John de Wakerle (who appointed John de Bray, rector of Naunton (Gloucs.), as his substitute)	

---

[17] For the bishop of Winchester's execution of the parliamentary writ see *Reg. Woodlock*, pp. 155–6, and 194–5.

[18] And for the payment of expenses ('of the clerk of the deanery going to parliament') from the income of the church of Combe, in the archdeaconry of Winchester, see Morgan, *Lands of Bec*, p. 58 n. 5.

Parliament	Diocese/archdeaconry or cathedral chapter	Names of proctors	Source
1307 13 Oct.[19] Northampton	Prior and chapter of Canterbury	Guy de Smeredenn' and Gilbert de Bisshoppestone, monks	Parl. Writs, II. ii. 3 (from CUL, Ee.v.31, fo. 107v)
	Clergy of Bath and Wells diocese	M. Hugh de Pencryz and M. Robert Fayrmay	SC10/1/20, see Appendix 1(a)
	Prior and chapter of Ely	Robert de Swafham, monk	SC10/1/27
	Clergy of Shropshire archdeaconry	Walter, vicar of Cleobury Mortimer (Salop), and M. John de Brunsope, rector of Oldbury (Salop)	SC10/1/28, see Appendix 1(b)
	Clergy of Carlisle diocese	M. William de Brampton, M. Adam de Appelby and Hugh de Burgo	Reg. Halton, II. 234 (from SC10/1/29)
	Clergy of York diocese	M. John de Snaynton, rector of Rudston (Humberside), and William de Pykering, rector of Hawksworth (Notts.)	SC10/1/30
	Clergy of Ely diocese	M. Richard de Otryngham and M. Robert de Abynton', rector of Graveley (Cambs.)	SC10/1/33
	Chapter of Hereford	Walter of Logwardyn	SC10/1/35
	Clergy of Durham diocese	Roger Bertram, rector of Bothal (Northumb.), and Reginald de Stepilton, rector of Wolsingham (Durham)	SC10/1/38
	Chapter of St Paul's London	John de Dutone, canon	SC10/1/39
	Chapter of Wells	William de Bourn', canon	SC10/1/42
	Chapter of York	Adam de Osgoteby, John de Merkenfeld and Robert de Bardelby, canons	SC10/4/168

[19] All the proctors of the diocesan clergy noted here from the proxies are also listed on the verso of a portion of a roll which is a list of members for this parliament: PRO, C49/4/1. On 18 Sept. the bishop of Winchester referred (Reg. Woodlock, p. 207) to the next congregation of the clergy of the archdeaconry of Winchester for the purpose of electing a proctor for this parliament.

Parliament	Diocese/archdeaconry or cathedral chapter	Names of proctors	Source
1309 27 April[20] Westminster	Prior and chapter of Canterbury	Nicholas de Burn' and Thomas de Wynchelese, monks	Parl. Writs, II. ii. 26 (from CUL, Ee.v.31, fo. 111r)
	Clergy of Carlisle diocese	M. Adam de Appelby and Robert de Meburn, canon of Lanercost	Reg. Halton, I. 314
	Chapter of Rochester	Geoffrey de Mepham and Hamo de Heth', monks	SC10/1/48
	Clergy of Winchester archdeaconry	John de Malmesbur', rector of St Mary of the Valleys (Winchester)[21]	SC10/1/49A
	Clergy of St Asaph diocese	M. Howel ap Ithal and M. Richard de Albo Monasterio	SC10/2/51
	Chapter of Lincoln	Hugh de Normanton, canon, and M. Thomas de Langetoft, rector of ?Aston Rowant (Oxon.) or Easton on the Hill (Northants.)	SC10/2/54
	Clergy of Lewes archdeaconry	William de Loppedel, vicar of Preston (E. Sussex)	SC10/2/55
	Clergy of York diocese	[ ]estan and John Fraunceys, rector of Wheldrake (N. Yorks.)	SC10/2/56
	Chapter of Hereford	William de Mortuo Mari, canon, and M. [ ] de Orletone	SC10/2/57
	Clergy of Stafford archdeaconry	M. Geoffrey de Blaston, canon of Lichfield, and Robert, rector of Wolfhampcote (Warwicks.)	SC10/2/61
	Clergy of Hereford archdeaconry	M. Thomas de Olreton and M. Simon de Radenore	SC10/2/62
	Clergy of Bangor diocese	M. A., archdeacon of Anglesey, and M. Lewelmus	SC10/2/69A
	Clergy of Salop archdeaconry	M. Geoffrey de Blasten', canon of Lichfield, and M. [Robert],[22] rector of Wolfhampcote (Warwicks.)	PRO C270/35/17, see Appendix 1(c)

[20] Expenses paid to proctors of the clergy of Ely diocese for this parliament: Lowry, 'Clerical proctors', p. 449. In addition to the proxies in SC10 for this parliament see the proxy of the archdeacon of Stow (PRO, C49/45/2), printed in Weske, Convocation, p. 58 n. 10.

[21] For the payment of expenses, of the clerk going to parliament at London, from the income of the church of Combe, in the archdeaconry of Winchester, see Morgan, Lands of Bec, p. 58 n. 5.

[22] Gap left for name.

Parliament	Diocese/archdeaconry or cathedral chapter	Names of proctors	Source
1311 8 Aug. and 2 Dec.[23] London	Chapter of Norwich (for 8 Aug.)	[ ]	Norwich, D. & C. Muniments, Reg. IX, fos. 11v–12r[24]
	Prior and chapter of Canterbury (for 2 Dec.)	A. de Sandwic', monk	Parl. Writs, II. ii. 67 (from CUL, Ee.v.31, fo. 117v)
	Chapter of Worcester (for 2 Dec.)	Robert de Clifton, monk	Worcester, D. & C. Muniments, Liber Albus, fo. 51r (Lib. Alb., ed. Wilson p. 35)[25]
	Subprior and chapter of Bath (for 2 Dec.)	William de Hampton, monk	LI, Hale 185, fo. 114r (calendared in Bath Chartularies, ed. Hunt, pt 2, no 611)[26]
1312 20 Aug.[27] Westminster			
1313 18 March[28] Westminster	Dean and chapter of Bangor	David de Buelt	SC10/2/93
	Subprior and convent of Rochester	Hamo de Hethe, monk, and M. William de Fakenham	SC10/2/100, see Appendix 1(d)
	Chapter of St Asaph	M. Richard de Oswaldestre, canon	SC10/3/101
	Chapter of St Davids	M. Gilbert de Mosselwyk', archdeacon of Carmarthen, and Walter de Hyll', canons	SC10/3/107
1313 8 July Westminster	Chapter of Durham	M. John de Snaynton' and Geoffrey de Edenham	Durham, D. & C. Muniments, Reg. II, fos. 31v–32r
	Chapter of York	Adam de Osgotby and Robert de Bardelby, canons	SC10/3/126

[23] Summoned for 8 Aug. by king's 'premunientes' writ (Parl. Writs, II. ii. app. p. 37) and for 2 Dec. by archbishop's provincial writ (see above p. 19 and n. 5).
[24] Gemmipunctus in place of names. Also, separate abbreviated proxy of prior of Norwich, without names.
[25] Followed (fo. 51v) by proxy (also addressed to king) from the prior, who named Robert de Clifton and M. Thomas de Teffonte. A proxy of the chapter had been drawn up, naming Robert de Clifton, for 8 Aug.: Worcester, D. & C. Muniments, Liber Albus, fo. 50r (Lib. Alb., ed. Wilson, p. 35), which contains this memorandum (following proxy of prior of Worcester naming John de Sancto Briavello): 'Procuratorium autem conventus habuit frater Robertus de Clifton' sub forma consueta et sigilla communi'. But these proxies for 8 Aug. were not delivered, for in the margin is written 'Ista procuratoria non tradebantur quia clerus vocatione regie absque mandato archiepiscopi non tenentur parere'. See Clarke, Representation, p. 132 and n. 1.
[26] Addressed to archbishop.
[27] Summoned on 3 June for 23 July at Lincoln (prorogued 8 July to Westminster). Durham, D. & C. Muniments, Reg. II, fos. 2v–3r, contains an undated proxy of the prior of Durham for the projected parliament at Lincoln naming Hugh de Monte Alto, monk, and M. John de Snainton, 'our clerk', followed by a proxy of the chapter of Durham dated 27 June, also for the parliament at Lincoln, naming Hugh de Monte Alto and William de Giseburn', monks.
[28] Proctors of the clergy of Durham diocese had apparently been sent to this parliament: Reg. Kellawe, I. 310.

Parliament	Diocese/archdeaconry or cathedral chapter	Names of proctors	Source
1313 23 Sept. Westminster	Chapter of Durham	Geoffrey de Edenham and Robert de Derlington', 'our clerks'	Durham, D. & C. Muniments, Reg. II, fo. 33r
	Chapter of Worcester	Robert de Clyfton', monk	Worcester, D. & C. Muniments, Liber Albus, fo. 61r (omitted in *Lib. Alb.*, ed. Wilson)[29]
1314 9 Sept.[30] York	Prior and chapter of Canterbury	W. de Norwyco, monk and cellarer	*Parl. Writs*, II. ii. 128 (from CUL, Ee.v.31, fo. 159r)
	Chapter of Worcester	Thomas de Evesham and Richard de Haukeslowe	Worcester, D. & C. Muniments, Liber Albus, fo. 65r (*Lib. Alb.*, ed. Wilson, p. 43)[31]
1315 20 Jan. Westminster	Prior and chapter of Canterbury	H. de Sancta Margar' and G. de Bishoppestone, monks	*Parl. Writs*, II. ii. 139 (from CUL, Ee.v.31, fo. 155v)
	Chapter of St Davids	M. Gilbert de Mosselwik' and Walter de la Hulle, canons	SC10/3/145
	Chapter of Carlisle	John de Crosseby and Robert de Santford	*Reg. Halton*, II. 234 (from SC10/3/146)
	Dean and chapter of York	Adam de Osgotby, Robert de Bardelby and John de Merkingfeld, canons	SC10/3/147
	Clergy of Rochester diocese	Robert, rector of Blessed Mary Hoo (Kent), and Peter de [Fangefosse], vicar of Yalding (Kent)	SC10/3/149
	Archdeacon and clergy of Carlisle diocese	Hugh de Burgo, rector of Brough (Cumbria), and Robert de Appelby, rector of [ ]	SC10/4/157, see Appendix 1(e) (noted in *Reg. Halton*, II. 235)
	Clergy of York diocese	M. William de Rothewell, rector of Normanton (W. Yorks.), and M. John de Snaynton, rector of Rudston (Humberside)	SC10/4/161
	Chapter of St Asaph	M. Richard de Oswaldestre, canon	SC10/4/162
	Subprior and chapter of Bath	Thomas de Malmesbury, monk	SC10/4/176

[29] Memorandum (following summons to parliament): 'Constitutus est procurator conventus frater R. de Clyfton' sub forma consueta cum data xiiii kal. Octobris anno domini mᵒ cccᵒ xiii, et frater J. de Sancto Brievello et magister Willelmus de Wodeford procuratores prioris in forma consueta et sub data eadem.' The next item but one is a letter dated at Worcester on 11 Nov., of Robert de C., proctor of the prior and chapter, appointing M. T. de Teffonth' as his substitute; despite its late date (the writs 'de expensis' for this parliament are dated 15 Nov.), this possibly refers to Robert de Clyfton' appointing a substitute as proctor in parliament.

[30] It was possibly for this parliament that expenses were paid from the churches of Langtoft and Baston for the proctors of the clergy of Lincoln diocese: Page, *Estates of Crowland*, p. 63.

[31] See also *Early Compotus Rolls*, ed. T. M. Wilson and C. Gordon (Worcs. Historical Soc, 1908), p. 39 (Expenditure of Bursar for 7/8 Edward II): 'In expensis R. de Haukeslowe euntis ad parliamentum apud Ebor' xls.'

Parliament	Diocese/archdeaconry or cathedral chapter	Names of proctors	Source
1316 27 Jan.[32] Lincoln	Chapter of Ely	M. Geoffrey de Pakenham, professor of canon law, and Gilbert de Grittone, rector of Bluntisham (Cambs.)	BL, Add. 41612, fo. 28v[33]
	Clergy of Rochester diocese	Peter de Fangefosse, vicar of Yalding (Kent), and William de Burton', vicar of Cobham (Kent)	SC10/4/181
	Subprior and chapter of Rochester	William de Dene and John Bernard	SC10/4/183
	Prior and chapter of Durham	J. de Outrewyk', monk, and Robert de Tymporon	SC10/4/191
	Chapter of York	John de Hustwatt, Robert de Cotingham and M. Nicholas de Ros', canons	SC10/4/193
	Chapter of St Asaph	M. Richard de Oswaldestre	SC10/4/195
	Chapter of Lincoln	M. Thomas de Langetoft', canon	SC10/5/203
	Chapter of St Davids	Matthew de Shireford, canon of Abergwili (Dyfed)	SC10/5/213
1318 20 Oct. York	Prior and chapter of Canterbury	G. de Bramton'	Parl. Writs, II. ii. 185 (from CUL, Ee.v.31, fo. 196v)
	Prior and chapter of Ely	M. Ralph Olyver, rector of Malton (Cambs.), and Henry Thrippelawe	SC10/5/245
	Clergy of Surrey archdeaconry	M. John de Malmesbury	SC10/5/247
	Clergy of Winchester archdeaconry	John de Mucheldenere, rector of Chilcombe (Hants.)	SC10/5/248
	Dean and chapter of Bangor	M. Howel ap Ithel, canon of St Asaph, and Richard de Melton, canon of Bangor	SC10/6/252
	Clergy of York diocese	M. John de Skyrne, rector of Marton (N. Yorks.), and M. John de Lutton', rector of half of Rillington (N. Yorks.)	SC10/6/255, see Appendix 1(f)
	Chapter of Winchester	John de Malmesbury	SC10/6/256
	Clergy of Durham archdeaconry	M. Elias de [Colsull'], rector of Seaham (Durham)	SC10/6/256A
	Clergy of Ely diocese	M. Ralph Oliveri, rector of Malton (Cambs.), and M. Henry Trippelawe	SC10/6/257[34]
	Chapter of Durham	Emericus de Lumley, monk	SC10/6/258

[32] An ecclesiastical council of the southern province met in Lincoln on 26 Jan. It is possible that often the same proctors of the southern clergy were appointed for the two assemblies: see next note. For the ecclesiastical council the prior and chapter of Canterbury named J. de Weston and W. Ledeberi, monks (Parl. Writs, II. ii. 155 and CUL, Ee.v.31, fo. 162r).

[33] The same proctors were appointed by the chapter, and in a separate letter by the prior, for the ecclesiastical council of 26 Jan.: BL, Add. 41612, fos. 28r–29r.

[34] For the expenses paid to the proctors of the clergy of Ely diocese, possibly for this parliament, see Lowry, 'Clerical proctors', p. 449.

Parliament	Diocese/archdeaconry or cathedral chapter	Names of proctors	Source
1319 6 May York	Prior and chapter of Canterbury	M. Adam Murymouth'[35] and G. de Bramton'	Parl. Writs, II. ii. 199 (from CUL, Ee.v.31, fo. 201r)
	Clergy of Gloucester archdeaconry	M. John de [ ]cothern'	SC10/6/263
	Clergy of Carlisle diocese	M. Robert de Southayk' and M. Henry de Rillington'	SC10/6/264 (noted in Reg. Halton, II. 235)
	Clergy of St Davids diocese	M. Philip, archdeacon of St Davids and professor of canon law, and William de la Roche	SC10/6/265
	Clergy of York diocese	M. Thomas de Cane and William de Twyforde	SC10/6/276
	Clergy of Durham diocese	M. Elias de Colsull', rector of Seaham (Durham), and M. Richard de Meburn'	SC10/6/289
	Chapter of Worcester	John de Sancto Briavello, monk, and Thomas de Evesham	SC10/6/290
	Chapter of York	John de Brotherton', chamberlain	SC10/6/293
	Chapter of St Davids	M. Philip, archdeacon of St Davids and professor of canon law	SC10/6/296
	Chapter of Durham	M. Richard de Eryum, professor of both laws, Emericus de Lummely, monk, and Robert de Tymparoun	SC10/6/299

[35] Adam Murimuth probably did not attend: above p. 74.

Parliament	Diocese/archdeaconry or cathedral chapter	Names of proctors	Source
1321 15 July[36] Westminster	Prior and chapter of Canterbury	William de Ledeb', monk	Parl. Writs., II. ii. 237 and Lit. Cant., I. 54−5 (both from Canterbury, D. & C. Muniments, Reg. L, fo. 131r), and CUL, Ee.v.31, fo. 222v
	Dean and chapter of Wells	M. John de Bruton and M. Richard de Plumstock, canons	HMC, Calendar of MSS of D. & C. of Wells, I. 195
	Chapter of Norwich	Ralph de Moueslee and J. de Clipesby, monks	Norwich, D. & C. Muniments, Reg. IX, fo. 31r[37]
	Clergy of Winchester archdeaconry	M. Nicholas de Middeltone	Reg. Asserio, pp. 424−5[38]
	Chapter of St Asaph	M. Hugh ap Ithel	SC10/7/308
	Chapter of Worcester	M. John Geraud	SC10/7/318 and Worcester, D. & C. Muniments, Liber Albus, fo. 101r (Lib. Alb., ed. Wilson, p. 71)[39]
	Prior and chapter of Ely	John de Conigton', monk, and M. Henry de Thrippelowe	SC10/7/325, see Appendix 1(g)
	Subprior and chapter of Bath	M. John de Schoredich, professor of civil law	SC10/7/335
	Clergy of York diocese	M. John de Nassington, rector of Kirkton (alias Screveton, Notts.), and William de Wyntringham, rector of St George's (York)	SC10/7/336

[36] This parliament was attended in person by the dean of Lichfield, who, summoned by the archbishop of Canterbury, left Lichfield on 6 July and returned on 14 Aug.: Bodl., Ashmole 794, fo. 1r. The bishop of Salisbury did not send his certificate of execution of the summons to the archbishop 'eo quod mandatum predictum preiudiciale ut premittitur videbatur et alii episcopi ad mandatum predictum certificare noluerunt': Reg. Martival, II. i. 347.

[37] Note also of a separate proxy from the prior 'sicut in procuratorio de capitulo'.

[38] Proctor named in letter concerning expenses.

[39] This proxy (original, and enregistered copy) was addressed to the king but was expressly in answer to the archbishop's citation. Also in Liber Albus, fo. 101r, the prior appointed two proctors, Thomas de Evesham and M. John Geraud, in two proxies, one addressed to the archbishop of Canterbury and the other addressed to the king.

Parliament	Diocese/archdeaconry or cathedral chapter	Names of proctors	Source
1322 2 May[40] York	Prior and chapter of Canterbury	M. A. de Brugg' and M. Richard de Brenchesle	Parl. Writs, II. ii. 247 (from CUL, Ee.v.31, fo. 225v)[41]
	Chapter of Winchester	Geoffrey de Wyleford and John de ?Sycom	SC10/7/341
	Clergy of York diocese	M. John de Skyrne, rector of Marton (N. Yorks.), and M. Simon de Scanes, rector of half of Hutton Buscel (N. Yorks.)	SC10/7/349
	Clergy of Carlisle diocese	M. Robert de Suthayk' and M. Adam de Appelby	SC10/8/357 (noted in Reg. Halton, II. 235)
	Chapter of St Davids	M. David Fraunceys, rector of Johnstown (Dyfed)	SC10/8/358
	Subprior and chapter of Bath	Philip de Bathon'	SC10/8/361
	Clergy of the diocese of St Davids	M. David Fraunceys, rector of Johnstown (Dyfed), and Philip de Lawhadeyn, rector of Penboyr (Dyfed)	SC10/8/367
	Chapter of Worcester	Richard de Hauekeslowe and Henry de Ouleye	SC10/8/371 and Worcester, D. & C. Muniments, Liber Albus, fo. 105v (Lib. Alb., ed. Wilson, p. 73)[42]
	Subprior and chapter of Rochester	M. Thomas de Hethe, and John de Faversham, monk	SC10/8/380
	Chapter of York	M. John de Tinwell, vicar choral of York	SC10/8/381
	Chapter of Salisbury	M. John de Everdone, M. Robert de Worthe, canons, and M. William de Salton	SC10/8/384
	Chapter of Durham	John de Outrewyk' and John de A[ ]	SC10/8/388
	Prior and chapter of Ely	John de Coningtone, monk, and M. Nicholas de Stokton'	SC10/8/392

[40] Expenses paid for the proctors of the clergy of Ely diocese: Lowry, 'Clerical proctors', p. 449 and Page, Estates of Crowland, p. 63. Proctors of the clergy of some dioceses were certainly absent (and eight of the bishops from the southern province): Parl. Writs, II. ii. 259, Concilia, II. 515−16 and Reg. Martival, II. ii. 394−5.

[41] Memorandum of the appointments.

[42] Also proxy of the prior, appointing Thomas de Evesham and John de Evesham: Liber Albus, fo. 105r.

Parliament	Diocese/archdeaconry or cathedral chapter	Names of proctors	Source
1324 23 Feb. Westminster	Prior and chapter of Canterbury	William de Ledeburi, cellarer	*Parl. Writs*, II. ii. 294 (apparently from CUL, Ee.v.31, fos. 234v–235r)
	Chapter of Lichfield	M. Philip de Turwill', M. Gilbert de Bruera, Geoffrey de Eyton' and Thomas de Astel, canons	Bodl., Ashmole 794, fo. 7r[43]
	Chapter of Lincoln	M. John de Harington, M. Geoffrey de Eyton', M. William de Weston', canons, Robert de Luda, and Adam de Bisocampo	LAO, Lincoln D. & C. Archives, A/2/23, fo.2[44]
	Clergy of Dorset, Salisbury and Wiltshire archdeaconries	M. John de Tarente, rector of Berwick St John (Wilts.), and M. Walter de Houghton, rector of Sherston (Wilts.)	*Reg. Martival*, II. ii. 436[45]
	Clergy of Berkshire archdeaconry	M. John de Legh, rector of Uffington (Oxon.)	*Reg. Martival*, II. ii. 436[45]
	Chapter of Durham	Thomas de Hepscot' and John de Halnatheby	*Parl. Writs*, II. ii. 294 (from SC10/9/423)
	Chapter of Norwich	John de Clipsby, John de Berton', monks, and M. Adam de Flicham	*Parl. Writs*, II. ii. 295 (from SC10/9/432)
	Chapter of Carlisle	John de Capella de Karlio'	*Parl. Writs*, II. ii. 295 and *Reg. Halton*, II. 234 (both from SC10/9/435)
	Dean and chapter of York	M. Henry de Cliff' and M. Gilbert de Bruerio	*Parl. Writs*, II. ii. 294–5 (from SC10/9/437)
	Chapter of St Asaph	M. Richard [ ] and M. [ ]vychan	*Parl. Writs*, II. ii. 293 (from SC10/9/439)[46]
	Dean and chapter of Bangor	M. Madoc de Engelfeld' and M. David de Buelt'	*Parl. Writs*, II. ii. 293 (from SC10/9/443)
	Chapter of Worcester	Robert de Cliftone, monk	*Parl. Writs*, II. ii. 295 (from SC10/9/447)
	Clergy of Carlisle diocese	M. W. de Kendale, rector of Salkeld (Cumbria), and John de Mereborn', rector of Long Marton (Cumbria)	*Parl. Writs*, II. ii. 299 (from SC10/9/450, and noted in *Reg. Halton*, II. 235)

[43] Note of the election, of the first two named, at a meeting of the chapter on 15 Feb. 1324 and of the agreement to provide letters of proxy 'et adiungantur in litera Galfrid' de Eyton' et Thomas de Astel'.

[44] Geoffrey de Eyton, William de Weston and Adam de Byonchaumpe (*sic*) were appointed proctors for the ecclesiastical council which was to meet on 20 Jan. but was cancelled. After a note of the cancellation there is a copy of the proxy for the parliament of 23 Feb. naming John de Harington (proctor and 'presentium exhibitor'), followed by this statement: 'Id capitulum constituerunt quatuor alios procuratores videlicet magistros Galfrid' de Eyton' et Willelmum de Weston' concanonicos ipsorum, item dominum Robertum de Luda et Adam Bisocampo coniunctim et divisim.'

[45] Proctors named in a certificate following the elections.

[46] And the proctors noted (without names) in a mutilated list of attendance: *Parl. Writs*, II. ii. 311.

Parliament	Diocese/archdeaconry or cathedral chapter	Names of proctors	Source
1325 18 Nov. Westminster	Prior and chapter of Canterbury	J. de Maldone and S. de Sancto Petro, monks	Parl. Writs, II. ii. 335 (from CUL, Ee.v.31, fo. 244r)
	Chapter of Lincoln	M. John de Hagh, rector of Langton (?Lincs.), and M. John de Notingham	LAO, Lincoln D. & C. Archives, A/2/23, fo. 5, see Appendix 2
	Prior and chapter of Ely	Nicholas de Copmanford', monk, and M. William de Birton, rector of Newton (Cambs.)	SC10/10/475
	Chapter of Durham	Thomas Surtays and John de Halnatheby	SC10/10/476
	Chapter of St Davids	M. Stephen Nest, canon of Abergwili (Dyfed)	SC10/10/477
	Dean and chapter of Bangor	M. David de Buellt, canon	SC10/10/478
	Subprior and chapter of Winchester	Nicholas de Eneford, monk	SC10/10/487
	Chapter of York	M. Richard de Er[ime] and M. Richard de Baldock', canons	SC10/10/488
	Chapter of St Asaph	M. Matthew de Englefeld	SC10/10/491
	Subprior and chapter of Bath	John de Settenhampton	SC10/11/506
	Clergy of London archdeaconry	M. Hugh de Mortone, rector of Garsington (Oxon.) and official of the archdeacon of London, and M. Andrew de Offord, commissary general of the official	SC10/11/508
	Clergy of Rochester diocese	John Tilbon, vicar of Horton Kirby (Kent), and John de Brampton, vicar of East Greenwich (Kent)	SC10/11/509
	Chapter of Worcester	Thomas de Evesham	SC10/11/510
	Clergy of Durham diocese	Thomas de Bamburgh, rector of Ovingham (Northumb.), and John de Pollowe, dean of the prebendal church of Lanchester (Durham)	SC10/11/511
1327 7 Jan.[47] Westminster	Prior and chapter of Canterbury	Geoffrey Poterel, almoner, and Hugh de Byssopestone, archbishop's clerk	Parl. Writs, II. ii. 354
	Prior and chapter of Ely	Nicholas de Copmanford, monk, and M. William de Birton	BL, Add. 41612, fo. 69v

[47] Expenses apparently paid for proctors of the clergy of Ely diocese for this parliament: Lowry, 'Clerical proctors', p. 450. Twenty-one 'priests and clerks' were among those who swore an oath to support Queen Isabella and her son: see Clarke, Representation, pp. 181−2 and Calendar of Plea and Memoranda Rolls of London 1323−64, ed. A. H. Thomas (Cambridge, 1926), p. 14. Some of these were probably proctors of the lower clergy: M. William de Meleford had represented the clergy of the London diocese at Carlisle in 1307 (see above p. 105) and Richard de Chestre was to represent the chapter of York at the parliament of July 1328 (below p. 116).

Parliament	Diocese/archdeaconry or cathedral chapter	Names of proctors	Source
1327 15 Sept. [48] Lincoln	Prior and chapter of Canterbury	M. W. de Maydestan' and Thomas de Stowe	CUL, Ee.v.31, fo. 263v[49]
	Chapter of Durham	John de Outrewyke, monk	SC10/11/518
	Chapter of Lincoln	M. Thomas de Luda, treasurer	SC10/11/521
	Subprior and chapter of Coventry	John de Thoresby and Richard de Kyngton	SC10/11/522
	Chapter of Carlisle	M. Richard Pyioun	SC10/11/523
1328 7 Feb.[50] York	Chapter of Lichfield	M. Gilbert de Bruera	Bodl., Ashmole 794, fo. 18v[51]
	Dean and chapter of Bangor	Madoc, archdeacon of Anglesey, and M. Madoc de Egylfylde	SC10/11/513
	Chapter of Durham	John de Outrewyke, monk, and John de Halnatheby	SC10/11/539
1328 24 April[52] Northampton	Dean and chapter of York	M. Henry de Clyffe, John Gyffard and Nicholas de Hugate, canons	SC10/11/544
	Subprior and chapter of Rochester	M. William de Middeltone, vicar of Haddenham (Bucks.)	SC10/12/600A
1328 31 July York	Chapter of York	M. Richard de Cestr', M. Richard de Erime and John Giffard, canons	SC10/12/557
	Prior and chapter of Ely	M. William de Byrton' and M. Richard de Barton'	SC10/12/558
1328 16 Oct.[53] Salisbury	Clergy of Worcester archdeaconry	Thomas de Evesham	SC10/12/572
	Chapter of St Asaph	M. Richard de Oswaldestre, canon	SC10/12/577
	Dean and chapter of Bangor	Gernagius, rector of Llangian (Gwynedd)	SC10/12/583
	Prior and chapter of Ely	M. [ ] and M. [ ]	SC10/12/584
	Chapter of Norwich	M. Roger de Breus and William de Ayreminne	SC10/12/586
	Dean and chapter of York	M. Richard de Hardyngg, M. Richard de Eryum and John Gyffard, canons	SC10/12/590
1329 9 Feb. Westminster (adjourned session of previous parliament)	Chapter of St Asaph	Anian Loyt	SC10/12/599
	Dean and chapter of York	M. Henry de Cliff and and John Gyffard, canons	SC10/12/600

---

[48] Expenses paid for proctors of the clergy of Lincoln diocese and of Ely diocese for this parliament: Lowry, 'Clerical proctors', pp. 450–1.

[49] Memorandum of the appointment.

[50] Expenses paid for the proctors of the clergy of Lincoln diocese: Lowry, 'Clerical proctors', p. 450.

[51] The entry here strongly suggests, but does not prove, that Gilbert was the chapter's proctor at this parliament: 'Nonas Februar' concordatum fuit in capitulo in aula domini decani quod Gilbertus de Bruera iret apud Eboracum pro negotiis ecclesie.'

[52] Expenses paid for the proctors of the clergy of Lincoln diocese and of Ely diocese: Lowry, 'Clerical proctors', pp. 450–1.

[53] Expenses paid for the proctors of the clergy of Ely diocese: Lowry, 'Clerical proctors', p. 451.

Parliament	Diocese/archdeaconry or cathedral chapter	Names of proctors	Source
1330	Chapter of Worcester	Thomas de Evesham	SC10/13/608
11 March[54] Winchester	Dean and chapter of Bangor	William de Werdale, rector of Aberffraw (Gwynedd), and Robert de Biwell', rector of Aber (Gwynedd)	SC10/13/628
	Dean and chapter of York	M. Henry de Clyff', Gilbert de la Bruere and M. Nicholas de Ludlowe, canons	SC10/13/630
	Chapter of St Davids	M. Gruffinus Cantyton', canon	SC10/13/633
1330 26 Nov. Westminster	Prior and chapter of Durham	M. John de Hirlaw and M. John de Bekyngham	SC10/14/666
	Dean and chapter of Bangor	M. David de Buellt, canon	SC10/14/667
	Chapter of St Asaph	M. Richard de Oswaldestre, canon	SC10/14/674
	Clergy of Worcester archdeaconry	M. John de Lude	SC10/14/688
	Chapter of Worcester	Reginald de Evesham, rector of Kislingbury (Northants.), and John de Stoke, rector of Sedgeberrow (Heref. & Worc.)	SC10/14/693
	Clergy of Durham archdeaconry	M. John de Bekyngham	SC10/14/694, see Appendices 1(h) and 3
	Subprior and chapter of Coventry	M. John de Thoresby, John dictus de Sutham, monk, and Henry de Shulton'	SC10/14/695
	Clergy of Northumberland archdeaconry	M. John de Hyrlawe	SC10/14/696
1331 30 Sept. Westminster	Clergy of Carlisle diocese	M. Adam de Appelby, rector of Caldbeck (Cumbria), and Robert de Tynpanrow, rector of Kirklinton (Cumbria)	SC10/15/701
	Chapter of Worcester	Reginald de Evesham, rector of Kislingbury (Northants.)	SC10/15/705
	Dean and chapter of Bangor	M. David de Buellt, canon	SC10/15/720
	Chapter of St Asaph	M. Louis, archdeacon of St Asaph and canon	SC10/15/721

[54] Expenses were apparently paid to the proctors of the clergy of Ely diocese for this parliament: Lowry, 'Clerical proctors', p. 451. Atterbury wrote, Rights, Powers and Privileges, p. 570, citing the register of Ralph of Shrewsbury, bishop of Bath and Wells: 'Capitulum Wellense mittit unum, item Bathoniense alterum procuratorem ad parliamentum apud Wynton die dominica proxima ante festum sancti Gregorii.' But this assumption seems to be based solely on the note of the execution by the bishop of Bath and Wells of the king's summons: SRO, Reg. Shrewsbury, fo. 14v. There is also a note of the execution of the archbishop's summons for the ecclesiastical council of the same date: see fo. 17v.

Parliament	Diocese/archdeaconry or cathedral chapter	Names of proctors	Source
1332 16 March[55] Westminster	Prior and chapter of Ely	Nicholas de Coppinamford', monk, and M. Nicholas de Stocton'	SC10/15/742
	Chapter of St Asaph	M. Matthew de Trefvaur, canon	SC10/16/754
	Dean and chapter of York	M. Henry de Clyfe, John Gyffard' and Robert de Valoignes, canons	SC10/16/766
	Clergy of Carlisle diocese	Adam de Dalton, prior of Wetheral (Cumbria), and Robert de Tymperon, rector of Kirklinton (Cumbria)	SC10/16/771
	Chapter of Lincoln	M. Simon de Islep, archdeacon of Stow, M. William Bacheler and Richard de Whitewelle, canons	SC10/16/788
1334 21 Feb. York	Dean and chapter of Bangor	M. David, archdeacon of Bangor, and Thomas de Capenhurst'	SC10/17/849
	Clergy of York diocese	M. Richard de Snoweshull', rector of Huntington (N. Yorks.), and M. William de Neusom', advocate of the court of York	SC10/17/849A
	Chapter of Worcester	Thomas de Evesham and Peter de Grete	SC10/18/854
	Chapter of Carlisle	John de Byghton', canon	SC10/18/856
	Clergy of Northumberland archdeaconry	M. Ralph de Blaykeston'	SC10/18/858
	Subprior and chapter of Coventry	Henry de Shulton' and William de Cestria	SC10/18/859
	Clergy of Carlisle diocese	Robert Coyvile, rector of Thursby (Cumbria), and M. John de Hakthorp'	SC10/18/862
	Chapter of St Asaph	Louis de Bromfeld', canon	SC10/18/864
	Chapter of Rochester	Thomas le Hoy and John de Faveresham	SC10/18/867
	Clergy of Durham archdeaconry	M. William de Vallibus	SC10/18/870

[55] See *Lit. Cant.*, I. 438–43, for correspondence between the prior of Canterbury and the archbishop of Canterbury concerning the procedure for summoning the chapter of Canterbury to this parliament.

Parliament	Diocese/archdeaconry or cathedral chapter	Names of proctors	Source
1334 19 Sept.[56] Westminster	Dean and chapter of Bangor	David, archdeacon of Bangor, and Gruffinus ap Tudur, canon	PRO C219/5/17/3[57]
	Clergy of York diocese	M. John de Thoresby, canon of Southwell (Notts.), and M. John de Barneby, rector of Barnby Dun (S. Yorks.)	C219/5/17/7
	Prior and chapter of Carlisle	David de Wolhore, rector of Knarsdale (Northumb.)	C219/5/17/12
	Clergy of Northumberland archdeaconry	William [de] Emyldon and John Wawayn	C219/5/17/15
	Chapter of Worcester	Thomas de Evesham	C219/5/17/25, see Appendix 1(i)
	Clergy of Worcester diocese	M. William de Adel[ynton'] and Thomas de Donynton, vicar of Grafton (Heref. & Worc.)	C219/5/17/26
1335 26 May York	Clergy of Carlisle diocese	M. Thomas de Halghton', rector of Kirkland (Cumbria), and Richard de Craystok', vicar of Crosthwaite (Cumbria)	SC10/19/901
	Chapter of St Asaph	Thomas de Capenhurst'	SC10/19/903
	Dean and chapter of Bangor	M. David, archdeacon of Bangor, and Thomas de Cappenhurst	SC10/19/906
	Chapter of Worcester	John de Dombelton, rector of Sedgeberrow (Heref. & Worc.)	SC10/19/910
	Prior and chapter of Ely	Robert de Aylesham, monk, and Henry de Theff'	SC10/19/915 and BL, Add. 41612, fo. 73r
	Chapter of Durham	M. Robert de Neunham	SC10/19/929, see Appendix 1(j)
	Clergy of York diocese	M. Richard de Wath, advocate of the court of York, and Robert de Ruddeby, rector of Goxhill (Humberside)	SC10/19/934
	Chapter of York	M. Richard de Haveryng', John Gyffard' and Nicholas de Hongate, canons	SC10/19/940
	Clergy of Durham archdeaconry	M. William de Alverton', vicar of Aycliffe (Durham)	SC10/19/944, see Appendix 1(k)

[56] Expenses paid for the proctors of the clergy of the Ely diocese, for this or the following parliament: Lowry, 'Clerical proctors', p. 451. An ecclesiastical council of the southern province met at St Paul's on 19 and 26 Sept. Some, if not most, of the proctors for these assemblies were no doubt the same as for the parliament; one of the two from the Worcester diocese was certainly the same. The following proctors for the ecclesiastical council are known. Prior and chapter of Canterbury: Simon de Sanco Petro, monk, and M. Simon de Cheringg', rector of Deal (Kent): Canterbury, D. & C. Muniments, Reg. L, fo. 37v (noted in Atterbury, *Rights, Powers and Privileges*, p. 571). Clergy of Worcester diocese: M. Richard Maynel', rector of Preston on Stour (Warwicks.), official of archdeacon of Worcester, and M. William de Adelynton', official of archdeacon of Gloucester: HWRO, Reg. Montacute, pp. 144–5 (named in schedule attached to certificate of execution). Clergy of Exeter diocese: Thomas and William de Nassington, canons: *Reg. Grandisson*, p. 766 (letter concerning their expenses). Also, the prior of Norwich appointed R. de D., monk: Norwich, D. & C. Muniments, Reg. X, fos. 1v–2r.

[57] C219/5/17 is a file of a total of 26 ecclesiastical proxies for this parliament, mostly from abbots.

Parliament	Diocese/archdeaconry or cathedral chapter	Names of proctors	Source
1336 11 March[58] Westminster	Clergy of York diocese	M. John de Burton, rector of Stokesley (N. Yorks.), and M. John de Barneby, rector of Barnby Dun (S. Yorks.)	SC10/18/875
	Dean and chapter of York	John de Warrenna, Robert de Valoygnes and M. Thomas [ ], canons	SC10/18/876
	Clergy of Northumberland archdeaconry	M. Ralph de Blaykiston'	SC10/18/879
	Clergy of Durham archdeaconry	[ ] Marmyon', rector of Houghton-le-Spring (Tyne & Wear)	SC10/18/886
	Chapter of Worcester	Simon Crompe, sacrist	SC10/18/894
	Chapter of St Asaph	[ ]	SC10/19/950
1336 23 Sept. Nottingham	Chapter of St Asaph	Thomas de Capenhurst, canon	SC10/20/961
1337 (9 Feb. York, prorogued to) 3 Mar. Westminster	Prior and chapter of Ely	W. de Lond' and Henry de Theford (for 9 Feb.)	BL, Add. 41612, fo. 81v
	Chapter of Worcester	Thomas de Evesham	SC10/20/957
	Clergy of Durham archdeaconry	John de Thoresby, rector of Elwick (Cleveland)	SC10/20/969
1337 26 Sept.[59] Westminster			
1338 3 Feb. Westminster	Prior and chapter of Canterbury	M. Simon de Cheryngg', rector of Deal (Kent)	Canterbury, D. & C. Muniments, Reg. L, fo. 105v (noted in Atterbury, *Rights, Powers and Privileges*, p. 571)
	Chapter of St Asaph	Thomas de Cappenhurst', canon	SC10/21/1008

[58] An ecclesiastical council of the southern province met at St Paul's on 11 March, and the clergy's proctors were no doubt often the same as for the parliament. The following proctors of the lower clergy for the council are known. Prior and chapter of Canterbury: M. Adam Merymouth, precentor of Exeter, Robert Hathebrand', monk, and Simon Cheryngg': Canterbury, D. & C. Muniments, Reg. L, fo. 43v (noted in Atterbury, *Rights, Powers and Privileges*, p. 571). Clergy of Worcester diocese: M. J. de Orleton, archdeacon of Worcester, for Worcester archdeaconry, and M. William de Adylmynton', for Gloucester archdeaconry: HWRO, Reg. Montacute, p. 172 (proctors named in schedule attached to certificate of execution). Prior and chapter of Ely: M. Laurence Fastolf and Robert de Aylesham, monk: BL, Add 41612, fo. 75r. Subprior and chapter of Norwich: Robert of Ely, monk, rector of Sudbury (Suff.) (name of rector not given), and Thomas de Bisele: Norwich, D. & C. Muniments, Reg. X, fo. 7v. Also, proxy of prior of Norwich (Reg. X, fo. 7): Robert de Ely, monk, John de Wymbotisham, rector of Polstead (Suff.), and Thomas de Brisele.

[59] An ecclesiastical council of the southern province opened at St Paul's on 30 Sept., and the following proctors are known. Chapter of Ely: Robert de Aylesham, monk. Clergy of Ely diocese: M. John de Tybenham and M. Robert de Brigham. These proctors are named in the certificate sent to the archbishop of Canterbury: CUL, EDR, Reg. Montacute, fo. 38v, and for brief note of bishop's execution of royal writ for parliament of 26 Sept. see fo. 70.

Parliament	Diocese/archdeaconry or cathedral chapter	Names of proctors	Source
1338 26 July[60] Northampton			
1339 3 Feb. Westminster	Prior and chapter of Canterbury	M. Thomas de Cant', rector of Great Buckland (Kent)	Canterbury, D. & C. Muniments, Reg. L, fo. 73r[61]
	Chapter of York	M. Thomas Sampson and John de Sancto Paulo, canons	SC10/21/1032
1339 13 Oct. Westminster	Chapter of Canterbury	M. Thomas de Cant'	Canterbury, D. & C. Muniments, Reg. L, fo. 74r[62]
	Chapter of York	John Gyffard, John de Sancto Paulo and John de Wodehous', canons	SC10/21/1040
	Chapter of Worcester	Simon Crumpe, sacrist	SC10/22/1063
	Clergy of York diocese (presenting excuses for absence)	M. Thomas de Harpham, advocate of the court of York, and M. Robert de Newenham, proctor of the court of York	SC10/22/1064
1340 20 Jan. Westminster	Clergy of York diocese (presenting excuses for absence)	M. William de Kendale and M. Robert de Neuwenham	SC10/21/1025
	Dean and chapter of Bangor	Henry de E[ ]lthale, rector of Caernarvon (Gwynedd), and ?Kyff-north de Grion	SC10/22/1081
1340 29 March Westminster	Chapter of St Asaph	M. Richard de Oswaldestre and M. Thomas de Capenhurst', canons	SC10/21/1036
	Chapter of York	John Gyffard, M. Thomas Sampson, John de Sancto Paulo and John Wodhouse, canons	SC10/22/1086
	Chapter of Worcester	Thomas de Evesham and Henry Geraud	SC10/22/1090
	Clergy of York diocese (presenting excuses for absence)	M. Robert de Newenham and M. John de Aslakby	SC10/22/1098, see Appendix 1(l)

[60] Expenses paid apparently for this and the following parliament for proctors of clergy of Ely diocese: Lowry, 'Clerical proctors', p. 452.
[61] Also separate proxy for prior naming same proctor.
[62] Memorandum of separate letters for chapter and for prior appointing the same proctor.

Select Bibliography

As a general rule works cited more than once in footnotes have been included in this bibliography. Primary material can be found in the first list through the abbreviated titles used in the footnotes; all secondary works appear, in the second list, under the authors' names.

Primary Sources

Bath Chartularies, ed. Hunt: *Two Chartularies of Bath*, ed W. Hunt (Somerset Record Soc., 7, 1893)

Bracton, ed. Woodbine: *Bracton de Legibus et Consuetudinibus Angliae*, ed. G. E. Woodbine (New Haven, 4 vols., 1915−42)

Brief Register, ed. Prynne: W. Prynne, *A Brief Register, Kalender and Survey of the Several Kinds, Forms of all Parliamentary Writs* (London, 4 vols., 1659−64)

Concilia: D. Wilkins, *Concilia Magnae Britanniae et Hiberniae* (London, 4 vols., 1737)

Councils and Synods II: *Councils and Synods II 1205−1313*, ed. F. M. Powicke and C. R. Cheney (Oxford, 2 vols., 1964)

Dignity of a Peer: *Reports from the Lords' Committees . . . touching the Dignity of a Peer* (London, 5 vols., 1820−9)

Early Rolls of Merton, ed. Highfield: *The Early Rolls of Merton College Oxford*, ed. J. R. L. Highfield (Oxford Historical Soc., new ser. 18, 1964)

Foedera: *Foedera, Conventiones, Litterae*, ed. T. Rymer (Record Commission, 3 vols. in 6, 1816−30)

Historical Papers, ed. Raine: *Historical Papers and Letters from the Northern Registers*, ed. J. Raine (RS, 1873)

Liber Albus, ed. Wilson: *Liber Albus of the Priory of Worcester*, ed. J. M. Wilson (Worcestershire Historical Soc., 1919)

Lit. Cant.: *Literae Cantuarienses*, ed. J. B. Sheppard (RS, 3 vols., 1887—9)

Parliamentary Texts, ed. Pronay and Taylor: N. Pronay and J. Taylor, *Parliamentary Texts of the Later Middle Ages* (Oxford, 1980)

Parl. Writs: *Parliamentary Writs and Writs of Military Summons*, ed. F. Palgrave (Record Commission, 2 vols. in 4, 1827—34)

Reg. Asserio: see *Reg. Sandale*

Reg. Baldock: *Registrum Radulphi Baldock, Gilberti Segrave, Ricardi Newport et Stephani Gravesend 1304—38*, ed. R. C. Fowler (CYS, 1911)

Reg. Bransford: *A Calendar of the Register of Wolstan de Bransford 1339—49*, ed. R. M. Haines (Worcestershire Historical Soc., and HMC Joint Publication 9, 1966)

Reg. Cobham: *The Register of Thomas de Cobham 1317—27*, ed. E. H. Pearce (Worcestershire Historical Soc., 1930)

Reg. Corbridge: *The Register of Thomas of Corbridge, Archbishop of York 1300—04*, ed. W. Brown and A. Hamilton Thompson (Surtees Soc., 2 vols., 1925—8)

Reg. Gandavo: *Registrum Simonis de Gandavo 1297—1315*, ed. C. T. Flower and M. C. B. Dawes (CYS, 1934)

Reg. Geynesborough: *The Register of William de Geynesborough 1302—07*, ed. J. W. Willis Bund (Worcestershire Historical Soc., 1907—29)

Reg. Giffard: *The Register of Godfrey Giffard 1268—1301*, ed. J. W. Willis Bund (Worcestershire Historical Soc., 2 vols., 1902)

Reg. Grandisson: *The Register of John de Grandisson 1327—69*, ed. F. C. Hingeston-Randolph (London, 3 vols., 1894—9)

Reg. Gravesend: see *Reg. Baldock*

Reg. Greenfield: *The Register of William Greenfield, Archbishop of York 1306—15*, ed. W. Brown and A. Hamilton Thompson (Surtees Soc., 5 vols., 1931—40)

Reg. Halton: *The Register of John de Halton 1292—1324*, ed. W. N. Thompson (CYS, 2 vols., 1913)

Reg. Hethe: *Registrum Hamonis Hethe 1319—52*, ed. C. Johnson (CYS, 2 vols., 1948)

Reg. Kellawe: *Registrum Palatinum Dunelmense: the Register of Richard de Kellawe 1314—16*, ed. T. D. Hardy (RS, 4 vols., 1873—8)

Reg. Martival: *The Registers of Roger Martival 1315—30*, ed. K. Edwards *et al.* (CYS, 4 vols., 1959—75)

Reg. Melton: *The Register of William Melton 1317—40*, ed. R. M. T. Hill *et al.* (CYS, 2 vols., 1977—8)

Reg. Orleton: *Registrum Ade de Orleton 1317—27*, ed. A. T. Bannister (CYS, 1908)

Reg. Pontissara: *Registrum Johannis de Pontissara 1282—1304*, ed. C. Deedes (CYS, 2 vols., 1915—24)

Reg. Romeyn: *The Register of John le Romeyn, Archbishop of York 1286—96*, ed. W. Brown (Surtees Soc., 2 vols., 1913—17)

Reg. Sandale: *The Registers of John de Sandale and Rigaud de Asserio 1316—23*, ed. F. J. Baigent (Hampshire Record Soc., 1897)

Reg. Sede Vacante: *The Register of the Diocese of Worcester during the Vacancy of the See, usually called Registrum Sede Vacante, 1301—1435*, ed. J. W. Willis Bund (Worcestershire Historical Soc., 1897)

Reg. Shrewsbury: *The Register of Ralph of Shrewsbury 1329—63*, ed. T. S. Holmes (Somerset Record Soc., 2 vols., 1896)

Reg. Stapeldon: *The Register of Walter de Stapeldon 1307—26*, ed. F. C. Hingeston-Randolph (London, 1892)

Reg. Sutton: *The Rolls and Registers of Oliver Sutton 1280—99*, ed. R. M. T. Hill (Lincoln Record Soc., 7 vols., 1948—75)

Reg. Wickwane: *The Register of William Wickwane, Archbishop of York 1279—85*, ed. W. Brown (Surtees Soc., 1907)

Reg. Winchelsey: *Registrum Roberti Winchelsey 1294—1313*, ed. R. Graham (CYS, 2 vols., 1952—6)

Reg. Woodlock: *Registrum Henrici Woodlock 1305—16*, ed. A. W. Goodman (CYS, 2 vols., 1940—1)

Return of Members: *Return of Every Member of the Lower House of the Parliaments of England, Scotland and Ireland . . . 1213—1874* (by order of the House of Commons, 2 vols., 1878)

Rot. Parl.: *Rotuli Parliamentorum* (Record Commission, 6 vols., 1783)

Rot. Parl. Inediti: *Rotuli Parliamentorum Anglie Hactenus Inediti*, ed. H. G. Richardson and G. Sayles (Camden Soc., 3rd ser. 51, 1935)

Sext: *Liber Sextus Decretalium Bonifacii VIII* in *Corpus Iuris Canonici*, ed. E. Friedberg (Leipzig, 2 vols., 1879—81), II. 937—1124.

Statutes: *Statutes of the Realm* (Record Commission, 11 vols. in 12, 1810—28)

Summa Artis Notarie: John of Bologna's *Summa Artis Notarie* in *Briefsteller und Formelbücher des elften bis vierzehnten Jahrhunderts*, ed. L. Rockinger, II (*Quellen und Erörterungen zur Bayrischen und Deutschen Geschichte*, IX², 1864), pp. 605—20

BIBLIOGRAPHY

Taxatio: *Taxatio Nicholai IV*, ed. T. Astle *et al*. (Record Commission, 1802)
Vita Ed.II, ed. Denholm-Young: *Vita Edwardi Secundi*, ed. N. Denholm-Young (London, 1957)

Secondary Works

Aston, M., *Thomas Arundel* (Oxford, 1967)
Atterbury, F., *The Rights, Powers and Privileges of an English Convocation* (London, 1701)
Brown, E.A.R., 'Philip the Fair, *plena potestas* and the *aide pur fille marier* of 1308' in *Studies Presented to the International Commission for the History of Representative and Parliamentary Institutions*, 39 (1970), pp. 3 — 27
———— 'Representation and agency law in the later middle ages', *Viator*, 3 (1972), 329 — 64
Buck, M., *Politics, Finance and the Church in the Reign of Edward II: Walter Stapeldon, Treasurer of England* (Cambridge, 1983)
Cam, H.M., 'The community of the shire and the payment of its representatives in parliament', in *Liberties and Communities in Medieval England* (Cambridge, 1944), pp. 236 — 50
Cheney, C.R., *Notaries Public in England in the Thirteenth and Fourteenth Centuries* (Oxford, 1972)
———— 'Law and letters in fourteenth-century Durham: a study of Corpus Christi College, Cambridge, MS 450', *BJRUL*, 55 (1972 — 3), 60 — 85 (reprinted in *The English Church and its Laws 12th — 14th Centuries* (London, 1982))
Chew, H.M., *Ecclesiastical Tenants-in-Chief* (Oxford, 1932)
Clarke, M.V., *Representation and Consent* (London, 1936)
Cuttino, G.P., *Diplomatic Administration 1259 — 1339* (Oxford, 2nd edn 1971)
Davies, R.G., and Denton, J.H., (eds), *The English Parliament in the Middle Ages* (Manchester, 1981)
Denton, J.H., 'Walter Reynolds and ecclesiastical politics 1313 — 16' in *Church and Government in the Middle Ages: Essays to C. R. Cheney*, ed. C.N.L. Brooke *et al*. (Cambridge, 1976), pp. 247 — 74
———— 'The *communitas cleri* in the early fourteenth century', *BIHR*, 51 (1978), 72 — 8
———— *Robert Winchelsey and the Crown 1294 — 1313: a Study in*

the Defence of Ecclesiastical Liberty (Cambridge, 1980)

———— 'The clergy and parliament in the thirteenth and fourteenth centuries' in Davies and Denton (eds), *English Parliament*, pp. 88–108

Dooley, J.P., 'The Lower Clergy in Parliament 1295–1340' (Manchester M.A., 1980)

Edwards, J.G., 'The personnel of the Commons in parliament under Edward I and Edward II' in *Essays Presented to T. F. Tout*, ed. A. G. Little and F. M. Powicke (Manchester, 1925), pp. 197–214 (reprinted in Fryde and Miller (eds), *Historical Studies*, I. 150–67)

———— 'The *plena potestas* of English parliamentary representatives' in *Oxford Essays in Medieval History Presented to H. E. Salter* (Oxford, 1934), pp. 141–54 (reprinted in Fryde and Miller (eds), *Historical Studies*, I. 136–49)

Edwards, K., 'The political importance of English bishops during the reign of Edward II', *EHR*, 59 (1944), 311–47

Emden, A.B., *A Biographical Register of the University of Oxford to 1500* (Oxford, 3 vols., 1957–9)

———— *A Biographical Register of the University of Cambridge to 1500* (Cambridge, 1963)

Fryde, E.B., and Miller, E., (eds), *Historical Studies of the English Parliament* (Cambridge, 2 vols., 1970)

Gransden, A., *Historical Writing II, c. 1307 to the Early Sixteenth Century* (London, 1982)

Haines, R.M., *The Church and Politics in Fourteenth-Century England: the Career of Adam Orleton c. 1275–1345* (Cambridge, 1978)

Harriss, G.L., *King, Parliament and Public Finance in Medieval England to 1369* (Oxford, 1975)

———— 'The formation of parliament, 1272–1377', in Davies and Denton (eds), *English Parliament*, pp. 29–60

Jones, W.R., 'Bishops, politics and the two laws: the *gravamina* of the English clergy, 1237–1399', *Speculum*, 41 (1966), 209–45

Kemp, E.W., *Counsel and Consent* (London, 1961)

Lowry, E.C., 'Clerical proctors in parliament and knights of the shire, 1280–1374', *EHR*, 48 (1933), 443–55

Lunt, W.E., 'The consent of the lower clergy to taxation during the reign of Henry III', in *Persecution and Liberty: Essays in Honor of G. L. Burr* (New York, 1931), 117–69

———— *Financial Relations of the Papacy with England to 1327* (Cambridge Mass., 1939)

———— *Financial Relations of the Papacy with England 1327–1534*

(Cambridge Mass., 1962)

Maddicott, J.R., 'Parliament and the constituencies, 1272—1377', in Davies and Denton (eds), *English Parliament*, pp. 61—87

McHardy, A. K., 'The representation of the English lower clergy in parliament during the later fourteenth century' in *Sanctity and Secularity: the Church and the World* (*Studies in Church History*, 10), ed. D. Baker (Oxford, 1973), pp. 97—107

McKisack, M., *The Parliamentary Representation of the English Boroughs during the Middle Ages* (London, 1932)

Michaud-Quantin, P., *Universitas: Expressions du Mouvement Communautaire dans le Moyen Age* (Paris, 1970)

Moorman, J.R.H., *Church Life in England in the Thirteenth Century* (Cambridge, 1955)

Morgan, M., *The English Lands of the Abbey of Bec* (Oxford, 1946)

Page, F.M., *The Estates of Crowland Abbey* (Cambridge, 1934)

Plucknett, T.F.T., 'Parliament' in *The English Government at Work 1327—1336*, I, ed. J. F. Willard and W. A. Morris (Cambridge Mass., 1940), pp. 82—128 (reprinted in Fryde and Miller (eds), *Historical Studies*, I. 195—241)

Post, G., *Studies in Medieval Legal Thought: Public Law and the State 1100—1322* (Princeton, 1964), cap. 3, '*Plena potestas* and consent in medieval assemblies' (revision of article in *Traditio*, 1 (1943), 355—408)

Powicke, F.M., 'Recent work on the origin of the English parliament' in *L'Organisation Corporative du Moyen Age à la Fin de l'Ancien Régime* (*Studies Presented to the International Commission for the History of Representative and Parliamentary Institutions*, 3, 1939), pp. 133—40

—— and Fryde, E.B., (eds) *Handbook of British Chronology* (Royal Historical Soc., 2nd edn 1961)

Prestwich, M., 'Parliament and the community of the realm in fourteenth-century England' in *Parliament and Community*, ed. A. Cosgrove and J. I. McGuire (Dublin, 1983), 5—24

Queller, D.E., *The Office of Ambassador in the Middle Ages* (Princeton, 1967)

Raynor, D., 'The forms and machinery of the "Commune petition" in the fourteenth century', *EHR*, 56 (1941), 198—233, 549—70

Richardson, H.G., and Sayles, G.O., 'The parliaments of Edward II', *BIHR*, 6 (1928), 71—88 (reprinted in Richardson and Sayles, *English Parliament*)

—— *The English Parliament in the Middle Ages* (London, 1981)

Roskell, J.S., 'The problem of the attendance of the lords in medieval parliaments', *BIHR*, 29 (1956), 153—204 (reprinted in Roskell, *Parliament and Politics*, I)

—— 'A consideration of certain aspects of the English *Modus Tenendi Parliamentum*', *BJRL*, 50 (1968), 411—42 (reprinted in Roskell, *Parliament and Politics*, I)

—— *Parliament and Politics in Late Medieval England* (London, 3 vols., 1981—3)

Sayers, J.E., *Papal Judges Delegate in the Province of Canterbury 1198—1254* (Oxford, 1971)

Sayles, G.O., 'Representation of cities and boroughs in 1268', *EHR*, 40 (1925), 580—5 (reprinted in Richardson and Sayles, *English Parliament*)

—— 'Parliamentary representation in 1294, 1295 and 1307', *BIHR*, 3 (1925—6), 110—15 (reprinted in Richardson and Sayles, *English Parliament*)

—— *The King's Parliament of England* (London, 1975)

Smith, A.L., *Church and State in the Middle Ages* (Oxford, 1913)

Strayer, J.R., 'Laicization of French and English society in the thirteenth century', *Speculum*, 15 (1940), 76—86 (reprinted in *Medieval Statecraft and the Perspectives of History*, ed. J. F. Benton and T. N. Bisson (Princeton, 1971), pp. 251—65)

Thompson, A.H., *The English Clergy and their Organization in the Later Middle Ages* (Oxford, 1947)

Wake, W., *The State of the Church and Clergy of England* (London, 1703)

Walsh, K., *A Fourteenth-Century Scholar and Primate: Richard FitzRalph in Oxford, Avignon and Armagh* (Oxford, 1981)

Weske, D.B., *Convocation of the Clergy* (London, 1937)

Wright, J.R., *The Church and the English Crown 1305—34: a Study based on the Register of Archbishop Walter Reynolds* (Toronto, 1980)

Index of Manuscripts

(References to the pages of this book are in italic numerals.)

London, British Library
    Add. 41612 (Reg. of Chapter of Ely): *110, 115, 119-20*
    Cotton Faust. A vi (Reg. of Prior of Durham): *101*
    Cotton Vesp. E xxi (Reg. of Peterborough Abbey): *23, 33, 56, 65, 83*
London, Lambeth Palace Library
    Reg. of Walter Reynolds: *20*
London, Lincoln's Inn Library
    Hale 185 (Reg. of Bath Priory): *25, 27, 65, 103, 108*
London, Public Record Office
    C49 (Chancery Parliamentary and Council Proceedings), 4/1: *48, 106*; 45/2: *107*; 46/28-41, 47/1: *11*; 68/4: *48*
    C153/1 (Vetus Codex): *45, 104*
    C219 (Writs and Returns of Members to Parliament), files between 2/1 and 6/5: *11, 14-15, 24, 95, 119*
    C270 (Chancery Ecclesiastical Miscellanea), 35/17: *11, 26, 90, 107*
    E159 (King's Memoranda Rolls), 88: *62*
    E175 (Parliamentary and Council Proceedings), 1/21: *48*
    SC9 (Parliament Rolls), 15: *104*
    SC10 (Parliamentary Proxies), files 1-22: *passim*

Norwich, Norfolk and Norwich Record Office, Dean and Chapter Muniments
    Reg. IX: *20, 32, 73, 108, 112*
    Reg. X: *23, 32, 119-20*

Oxford, Bodleian Library
    Ashmole 794 (Lichfield Chapter Act Book): *26, 82, 112, 114, 116*

Taunton, Somerset Record Office
    Reg. of Ralph of Shrewsbury: *20, 117*

Trowbridge, Wiltshire Record Office
    Reg. of Robert Wyvil: *23, 82*

Worcester, Dean and Chapter Library
    Liber Albus: *20, 26, 28, 37, 104, 108-9, 112-13*
    Sede Vacante Register: *31*
Worcester, Hereford and Worcester Record Office
    Reg. of Godfrey Giffard: *50*
    Reg. of Simon Montacute: *18, 20, 23, 82, 119-20*
    Reg. of Thomas Hempnall: *65*

General Index

All place names have been identified and given their modern spelling using the *Bartholomew Gazetteer of Britain*, compiled by O. Mason (1st edition, 1977), but for surnames the contemporary spelling has, for the most part, been retained. Bishops are usually indexed under the names of their dioceses. M. = Magister.

133

135

of, 32, 105
summons, *see* archbishops, clergy,
premunientes, and writs
Surrey: clergy of archdeaconry of,
10n, 31n, 105, 110; official of,
33n
Surtays, Thomas, 115
Sutham, John dictus de, 117
Suthayk', Robert de (M.), 105, 113
Swaffham, Hugh de (M.), 104-5
Swafham, Robert de, 106
Sycom(?), John de, 113

Tamworth and Tutbury (Staffs.),
rural dean of, 33n
Tarenta (Trenta, Tarente), John de
(M.), rector of Berwick St John,
104-5, 114
taxation: of clergy, 3, 5, 19, 53,
62-7, 69-70, 74-5, 78, 82-4, 86,
100; assessment for, 28n, 57, 61-2,
84; for expenses of proctors, 54-9
Teffonte (Teffonth), Thomas de
(M.), 108n, 109n
Testa, William, 45n
Thaneto, J. de, precentor of
Canterbury, 103-4
Theford (Theff'), Henry de, 119-20
Thompson, A.H., 4
Thoresby, John de (M.), canon of
Southwell, rector of Elwick, 70n,
116-17, 119-20
Thorntoft, William (de), 46, 104
Thornton Dale (N. Yorks.), church,
105
Thrippelowe (Trippelawe), Henry
(de) (M.), 94, 110, 112
Thurlow (Suff.), church, 105
Thursby (Cumbria), church, 118
Tickhill (Notts.), royal free chapel,
37
Tilbon, John, vicar of Horton Kirby,
115
Tinwell, John de (M.), 113
Trefvaur, Matthew de (M.), canon
of St Asaph, 118
Trenta, *see* Tarenta
Tudur, Gruffinus ap, canon of
Bangor, 119
Turwill', Philip de (M.), canon of
Lichfield, 114
Tutbury, *see* Tamworth
Tutington', William de, 104

Twyforde, William de, 111
Tybenham, John de (M.), 120n
Tychewell, Hugh de (M.), 105
Tymperon (Tymporon, Tymparoun,
Tynpanrow), Robert de, rector of
Kirklinton, 110-11, 117-18

Uffington (Oxon.), church, 114
universities, 5-7, 75. *See also* master

Vallibus, William de (M.), 118
Valoignes, Robert de, canon of
York, 118, 120
Vita Edwardi Secundi, 74-5

Wakerle, John de (M.), 105
Walmesford, Hugh de (M.), 105
Walter, vicar of Cleobury Mortimer,
90, 106
Warrenna, John de, canon of York,
120
Wath, Michael de, keeper of rolls of
Chancery, 36n, 101
Wath, Richard de (M.), advocate of
court of York, 73n, 119
Wawayn, John, 119
Wells: archdeacon of, 45; dean,
and chapter, 89, 104, 106, 112
Werdale, William de, rector of
Aberffray, 117
Westminster, *see* parliament
Weston, J. de, 110n
Weston', William de (M.), canon of
Lincoln, 114
Wetheral (Cumbria), prior, *see*
Dalton
Wheldrake (N. Yorks.), church, 105,
107
Whitchurch, Nicholas de, official of
Lincoln *sede vacante*, 103n
Whitewelle, Richard de, canon of
Lincoln, 118
Wigan (Gtr Manchester), vicar of, 86
Wigford (Lincoln), church, 33
William, rector of Silvington, 105
Wiltshire, clergy of archdeaconry of,
114
Winchelsey, Robert, archbishop of
Canterbury (1293/4-1313), 20, 22,
24-5, 36n, 45n, 47, 61, 63, 67-8,
79, 81, 87, 91
Winchester: archdeacon of, 55,
clergy of archdeaconry of, 31 & n,

141